LITURGY OUTSIDE LITURGY

DAVID W. FAGERBERG

LITURGY OUTSIDE LITURGY

DAVID W. FAGERBERG

LITURGY OUTSIDE LITURGY

The Liturgical Theology of Fr. Alexander Schmemann

CHORABOOKS
HONG KONG 2018

For Kaj & Jennifer and Catherine & Samuel
As they discover joy in the liturgy of their domestic Church

Table of Content

Foreword

Thirty-five years after the repose of Protopresbyter Alexander Schmemann there are those who claim to know the mind of Schmemann and even claim to know what he would say today, if he were still among us. However, I am doubtful that anyone can assume the mantle of Schmemann except the man himself through his writings and legacy. He remains to this day an active voice among us as a liturgist, theologian, preacher, and pastor. He continues to speak for himself to others and his influence is proving to be timeless.

Like David Fagerberg, I did not have the blessing of sitting as one of Fr Alexander's students. I came to know him through his books, taped homilies and those who cherished him as their teacher and confessor. However, I did have the great privilege of knowing his widow, Matushka Juliana, in her finals years, as she resided near her beloved St. Vladimir's Seminary in New York. She shared many stories including her husband's pure joy in being at the altar and his frustration with so much fuss and bother about those things that really don't matter in the end.

The preface to Fr. Alexander's book *The Eucharist* says much about his consistent thinking: it is *"not reform, adjustments and modernization that are needed so much as a return to that vision and experience that from the beginning constituted the very life of the Church."* I know of no other author or serious student of the work of Alexander Schmemann who has captured his prophetic vision with more clarity than David Fagerberg: Fr. Alexander's lucid brilliance and overall vision shine forth in the lectures and reflections chosen by him for this publication.

Still, although Fagerberg is grateful for the foundational influence of Fr. Alexander upon his own academic work as a liturgical theologian, he admits there remains much work to be done in interpreting and building upon Schmemann's great legacy. In particular, I think there is much work to be done by Orthodox churches and communities in continuing to honestly critique how well they are living our the gospel of Christ.

This book, will be gratefully received by those who knew Fr. Alexander Schmemann, and also by those who have come to know him posthumously through his written word and recorded voice. May it be blessed!

Archpriest Chad Hatfield,
President, St. Vladimir Orthodox Theological Seminary,
Yonkers, New York.

Introduction

This manuscript comes from five lectures given in January of 2017. Three of them were presented at the invitation of Peter Halldorf to a seminar on Alexander Schmemann at The Ecumenical Community of Bjärka-Säby and The Academy of St John in Sweden. Two of them were presented at the invitation of Samuel Rubenson, professor at the University of Lund, to a doctoral seminar and to a group of interested lay people. I have left them in the genre of oral presentation since that was their genesis.

They are published together here, but the reader will notice a gap between the three and the two. In the first three I have stayed as close to Fr. Alexander's material as possible; in the latter two my own perspective is released. I have therefore decided to place the Schmemann material first, and ask the reader to treat them as laying the foundation for my own work – a metaphor I employ below. Fr. Alexander's work was tremendously influential on me as a graduate student trying to come to terms with liturgical theology. At that time I searched his writings primarily for what he could teach me about this subject. Writing the talks for the seminar in Sweden gave me the opportunity to read in his corpus more widely, and I commenced by gathering as many of his other essays as I could find (there were quite a number I had overlooked in my required focus on the dissertation). It has been a deep and satisfying pleasure to let him tutor me again, this time on a wider array of subjects that are still somehow all connected, for this is a particular genius of his. To speak about liturgy we must speak about the Church; to speak about the Church we must speak about the world; but the world is in its course of transfiguration, so we are brought to examine our current lives through the eschatological gates to eternity.

I never had the opportunity to meet Fr. Alexander in person; he died the year I began my studies. There are many better books written by people who knew him, but I hope the reader will here profit from hearing his voice in the first three chapters. And any good things I can say about liturgy in the last two chapters seem somehow to trace back to him, even if not directly; any stumbles in them are, of course, mine.

David W. Fagerberg
Professor, Department of Theology
University of Notre Dame

Part I: A Sketch of Alexander Schmemann's Thought on Liturgy, Theology, and Piety

As much as possible we will convey Schmemann's varied attempts to connect liturgy, theology, and piety, and find his explanations about why this is important. It is the task, he says, of liturgical theology to reunite these three, but it is not just a personal opinion of his. I believe he finds ecclesiology at stake in the success.

Chapter 1: Should Liturgy Matter Outside the Church? Schmemann on the Study of Liturgy

Schmemann himself is responsible for the structure of my three talks. I don't mean he spoke to me in my sleep or met me over the Ouija board, I mean that I have long wished to explore one of his clearer statements about what liturgical theology is, and am grateful to this symposium for the opportunity to do so. I began by reimmersing myself in his thought by reading articles I had not previously read when I was more narrowly focused on my dissertation topic. It was a risk to return to an author who was so important to me over three decades ago – will I find him passé? will my interests have moved on? I'm happy to report that Schmemann is as stimulating and fruitful as he ever was.

In an exchange over some articles by Botte and Grisbrooke, Schmemann identifies where they, and others, have gone wrong in understanding him. They believe that he wants to "relegate the 'accessories' to their place," or "prepare grounds for a liturgical reform that would restore the 'essence' of the liturgy," and Schmemann responds that

this is not his concept of liturgical theology at all. Sensing the

potential exasperation of a reader, Schmemann concludes:

> "Finally one may ask: but what do you propose, what
>
> do you want? To this I will answer without much
>
> hope, I confess, of being heard and understood: we
>
> need liturgical theology, viewed not as a theology of
>
> worship and not as a reduction of theology to liturgy,
>
> but as a slow and patient bringing together of that
>
> which was for too long a time and because of many
>
> factors broken and isolated – liturgy, theology, and
>
> piety, their reintegration within one fundamental
>
> vision. In this sense liturgical theology is an
>
> illegitimate child of a broken family. It exists, or
>
> maybe I should say it ought to exist, only because
>
> theology ceased to seek in the *lex orandi* its source and
>
> food, because liturgy ceased to be conducive to
>
> theology."[1]

Schmemann tells us himself that the most characteristic thing about his thinking – the thinking we have gathered to explore – is the reunification of liturgy, theology, and piety. When the latter two are divorced from the former one, then theology "is imprisoned in its own 'data' and 'propositions,'" and having eyes does not see and having ears does not hear," and liturgical piety "is entangled in all kinds of liturgical experiences save the one expressed in the *lex orandi* itself."[2]

The three topics Schmemann identifies are supposed to be seen behind the questions I hid in the titles of my talks: (1) What is Schmemann's understanding of the study of liturgy, and should it matter outside the Church? (2) What is his concept of theology, and can it be done outside the academy? And (3) what is the connection he sees between liturgy and piety, i.e., do we need liturgy in our life?

We could go at it another way, based off a second quotation from Schmemann. In his book on baptism he describes his objective again.

"The goal of liturgical theology, as its very name indicates, is to overcome the fateful divorce between theology, liturgy and piety – a divorce which, as we have already tried to show elsewhere, has had disastrous consequences for theology as well as for liturgy and piety. It deprived liturgy of its proper understanding by the people, who began to see in it beautiful and mysterious ceremonies in which, while attending them, they take no real part. It deprived theology of its living source and made it into an intellectual exercise for intellectuals. It deprived piety of its living content and term of reference."[3]

Separate *liturgy* from theology and piety, and believers expect nothing but beautiful and mysterious ceremonies in which they take no real part. Separate *theology* from liturgy and piety, and it becomes an intellectual exercise for a privileged group of academics. Separate *piety* from liturgy and theology and it loses its living content and term of reference. These bricks should make up the house in which we live our Christian life, but we instead find a pile of rubble because the bricks are not connected.

I have found a third place where Schmemann takes a tour of that rubble. Isolate liturgy, and one might become a liturgical conservative who delights in the colorful rites of Byzantium as precious relics of a cherished past, but one will

"completely fail to see in them, in the totality of the Church's *leitourgia* and all-embracing vision of life, a power meant to judge, inform and transform the whole of existence, a "philosophy of life" shaping and challenging all our ideas, attitudes and actions. As in the case of theology, one can speak of an alienation of liturgy from life, be it from the life of the Church or the life of the Christian individual. Liturgy is confined to the temple, but beyond its sacred enclave it has no impact, no power. ... A liturgical pietism fed by sentimental and pseudo-symbolic explanations of liturgical rites results, in fact, in a growing and all-pervading secularism."[4]

How can we stitch these three elements together into Schmemann's wished-for full understanding of liturgical theology? How can the bricks be reconnected after falling apart?

Liturgy and the World

We will begin in this first talk by examining Schmemann's idea of liturgy vis-à-vis the world. Does liturgy make the world irrelevant to Christians? Does liturgy only matter to members of the Jesus Club when they get together to kill a Sunday morning? Is liturgy basically nothing more than temple etiquette, inessential to the mundane world? Should liturgy matter outside the Church? Such questions concern Schmemann a great deal, but we will find his answer involves a difficult concept of antinomy. He objects to a *reductionistic* view that downgrades *leitourgia* to nothing but cultic action; or perhaps we could call it a *restrictive* view because it limits liturgy to being a device in the Church to meet people's personal religious needs. We find ample documentation of this in Schmemann's writings, but will look at only three examples, sufficient to grasp how forcefully he shuts the door on this view of liturgy. Here is a first example, where he defines the error as thinking the Church exists for the sake of the cult, instead of vice versa:

> "The overwhelming majority of Orthodox people have no interest in the meaning of worship. ... The believer loves the ceremonies, symbols, the whole atmosphere of the Church building, this familiar impression is nourishment for his soul, but this love does not long for understanding, because the purpose of cult is thought of precisely as the bestowal of a spiritual experience, spiritual food. For the membership of the Church worship has ceased to be the Church's self-evidencing."[5]

Having become a "cultic society," that exists in and for the sake of the cult, we cannot understand how worship places the Church before the face of the world. This problem exists not only for the average parishioner, but for the average seminarian, as well. "It is not by chance that our own young churchly people turn back with such enthusiasm to cassocks, to clerical hats, to the whole clerical apparatus."[6]

Here is a second example in which Schmemann condemns the hypocrisy of a person who will be very religious but not let religion affect his or her life:

"A "secularist" is usually a very religious man, attached to his church, regular in attending services, generous in his contributions, acknowledging the necessity of prayer, etc. He will have his marriage "solemnized" in church, his home blessed, his religious "obligations" fulfilled, all this in perfect good faith. But all this will not in the least alter the plain fact that his understanding of all these spheres:

marriage, family, home, profession, leisure, and, ultimately, his religious "obligations" themselves, will be derived not from the creed he confesses in church, not from the Incarnation, Death, Resurrection and Glorification of Christ, the Son of God become Son of Man, but from philosophies of life …"[7]

And here is a final, lengthy example describing how people want to use the cult as a way to dispatch all their religious obligations:

"The question, which underlies the whole liturgical experience of Orthodoxy, "what does it reveal about me and my life, what does it mean for my activity and my relation to men, nature and time," is replaced little by little by an entirely different question: "how much of the liturgy is needed to put me in 'good standing'"? And where religion becomes a matter of obligation and good standing, there inevitably all questions concerning the "right" and the "wrong" practices acquire a kind of independence from their moral, existential, truly religious implications. The priest is satisfied if he celebrates the "correct" liturgy, the people are satisfied if they know exactly the amount of their religious obligations, the whole parish is proud of its beautiful church and beautiful services — but that which, from the very beginning was the real fruit of the Liturgy, … that challenge to my whole life, that call to perfection, that nostalgia for a change, a transformation, a transfiguration — all this is absent. The liturgy is still the center of our Church life, unquestioned, unchallenged, unopposed. But it is in fact a center without periphery, a heart with no control on blood circulation, a fire with nothing to purify and to consume, because that life which had to be embraced by it, has been satisfied with itself and has chosen other lights to guide and to shape it."[8]

These may seem like surprising quotes from a man reputed to be a defender of the liturgy. He objects to a fascination, obsession, enthrallment with the liturgy qua liturgy. He objects to an antiquarian fascination with a golden age, to being dazzled by the ceremonial, to being awed by the pageantry, when this is precisely the only thing we think fascinates a liturgical scholar. This approach goes wrong for isolating liturgy to a spiritual realm. In that case, religious life is considered irrelevant to our every day, secular, mundane world.

But if Schmemann objects to a restrictive understanding that confines liturgy to the temple, would he be any happier if we drove people out of the sacred into the streets so they could address the problems of the world? Does Schmemann follow the frequent dialectic that balances religiosity with social justice activity? We can guess the answer, since placing one error in opposition to another error rarely yields truth, but let's look at some examples anyway.

Schmemann does not recommend that the Church follow the world's lead.

> "The tragedy, then, is not the Church has failed to "understand" the world and to follow it in all its pseudo-metamorphoses. Rather, the tragedy lies in this: that she followed the world too much, adopting for the explanation of her faith philosophies and thoughts forms alien to it..."[9]

He does not think the Church should transform herself into one more agency of reform, a mistake the West made in its distinctive way, but a mistake we shall see tempts the Orthodox, as well.

> "The Western Church has understood its participation in the life of the world as a hierarchical power over the world. But when the world rejected that power, the Church resorted to direct participation in politics – first right, then left. ... The Church is gradually identified as one of the means in

the fight for freedom, equality and fraternity, for the defense of the third world, for any utopia inscribed on this and that banner."[10]

Why can't the Church simply join the forward evolutionary march toward improved conditions for mankind? Because the problem cuts deeper.

"'This world,' by rejecting and condemning Christ, has condemned itself; no one, therefore, can enter the kingdom without in a real sense dying to the world, i.e. rejecting it in its self-sufficiency...[11]

In this world Christ was rejected. ... He was the heartbeat of the world and the world killed him. But in that murder the world itself died. It lost its last chance to become the paradise God created it to be. We can go on developing new and better material things. We can build a more humane society which may even keep us from annihilating each other. But when Christ, the true life of the world, was rejected, it

was the beginning of the end."[12]

Schmemann is unimpressed with attempts to blend in with

the world, and he can be quite sarcastic about it in his

Journals.

"I am convinced that this phenomenal success [of

Pope John Paul II's visit to America in 1979] will not

make even one nun go back to wearing a robe. And I

have almost immediate proof: during lunch, five

Jesuits and one Franciscan ... are wearing elaborate

lay clothes, almost glaring with their multi-colored

ties, light suits, colored vests. ... Yesterday, during a

very friendly and genuinely disturbed discussion after

my lecture (about the Holy Spirit, the Liturgy,

Eschatology) these same Jesuits in bright ties ask:

"...yes but the world; where is the world? Where does

it connect with the world?""[13]

We are familiar with everything I've been quoting because it appears in the opening chapter of *For the Life of the World* in which Schmemann contrasts the spiritualist with the activist. The former would treat liturgy as a retreat from the world into spirituality, leaving the secular world without significance; the latter would take the world as an end in itself, treating liturgy as a wasteful distraction. If in its rejection of Christ the world has killed itself, then there is no advantage to the Church accompanying the world into the grave – unless, that is, it knew the way out of the tomb! It turns out that the liturgy *is* interested in the world: it is interested in the world's passage into the Kingdom of God. Schmemann does not want the liturgy to conform to the world, he wants liturgy to redeem it; he does not want the world to abandon liturgy, he wants it to be taken up into the liturgy. Liturgy and the world must be held together in paradoxical tension. Thus Schmemann rejects the choice between sacred liturgy or profane pragmatism, and instead offers an antinomy that binds them together. But antinomies are difficult, so let us roll up our sleeves.

Defining Antinomy

A couple definitions of antinomy might help, taken from Pavel Florensky's thesis *Pillar and Ground of the Truth*, a name Schmemann mentions in his introductory survey to Russian theology. Florensky says antinomy begins with the conviction that "life is infinitely fuller than rational definitions and therefore no formula can encompass all the fullness of life."[14] Truth is one; the form and content of Truth is one; but it is not known as one when perceived by a creature who lives in time and space. For the finite knower, "Knowledge *of* the Truth becomes knowledge *about* the Truth. And knowledge about the Truth is *truth*."[15] In God, Truth is one, but finite creatures know Truth as truths, and when scattered across the page the plurality of truths may seem to contradict each other. Antinomy is precisely going past this experience of contradictoriness to arrive at unity. "Antinomicalness does not say, 'Either the one or the other is not true.' It also does not say, 'Neither the one nor the other is true.' It only says, 'Both the one and the other are true, but each in its own way. Reconciliation and unity are higher than rationality.'"[16] Refusing antinomy is the root of heresy, *airesis*, which chooses one truth over another. Accepting antinomy is more than an act of the intellect, however, because the contradictions we face come not only from our finitude but also our fallenness. The mind is tempted to see by natural light alone, ignoring the spiritual light that shines from heaven, so the advance from contradictoriness to antinomy must be led by grace. Florensky concludes, "These contradictions are eliminated in the mind only at moments of illumination by grace. But they are eliminated not rationally but suprarationally. ... Only the purified God-bearing mind of saintly ascetics is *somewhat* more whole. In this mind, the healing of the fissures and cracks has begun; the sickness of being is being cured; the wounds of the world are being healed."[17] Apparently a dogma will be experienced differently by fallen rationality than by a reason that has been spiritually purified. Who would have thought that asceticism has something to do with epistemology?

Schmemann uses almost identical language to Florensky when he writes in his Journals "The sum of scientifically stated truths does not discover nor reveal *Truth*."[18] Chopping up Truth (singular and with a capital T) into scientific bits for the sake of specialization is what Schmemann calls the "Western captivity" inflicted upon Orthodoxy. The West brought topical and methodological fragmentation, and so it is necessary to learn how to reunite the truths into Truth. "If a certain degree of specialization is obviously necessary because it is beneficial to theology's scientific progress, this specialization not only does not exclude, but indeed requires as the very condition of its success and as its inner justification the convergence and interdependence of all disciplines as to their common source and their common goal."[19] And that common source and common goal of theology is the liturgy, precisely as an expression of the Church's *leitourgia*, which is an epiphany of her eschatological identity. "One can rightly describe the Church as an eschatological reality, for its essential function is to manifest and to actualize in this world the eschaton, the ultimate reality of salvation and redemption. In and through the Church the Kingdom of God is made already present, is communicated to men."[20]

Schmemann uses the word antinomy often, and I will classify those uses into two categories, the first concerning the Christian's relationship with the world, and the second concerning the eschatological character of liturgy.

First, the Christian's relationship with the world is an antinomy. "This struggle with history, which inevitably follows its course, comes from an inability to come to terms with the basic Christian antinomy: 'in this world, but not of this world' and to understand that the Orthodox world is of this world."[21] To translate into Florensky's definition, antinomicalness does not say either we are in the world or we are out of it; it also does not say we are neither in the world nor out of it; it only says, we are both in the world and not of it, each in its own way. Schmemann adds,

> "It is strange, indeed, that in our present preoccupation with the world we seem to ignore the fundamental antinomy traditionally implied in the Christian usage of that term. We seem to forget that in the New Testament and in the whole Christian tradition the "world" is the object of two apparently contradicting attitudes: an emphatic acceptance, a *yes*, but also an equally emphatic rejection, a *no*."[22]

The antinomy that lies at the foundation of Christian life is found in the fact that "the Christian is called to deny himself, to 'lay down his life for his friends'; and the same Christian is summoned to 'despise the flesh, for it passes away, but to care instead for the soul, for it is immortal.'"[23] The Christian gospel is antinomous for being directed to the whole world and at the same time turning to each human being, unique and unrepeatable. In order to save one, the shepherd left the ninety-nine, but the same Church cuts off sinners from herself for the sake of her purity and fullness. This is the first antinomy: to save the world, we must leave it.

The second antinomy surrounds the liturgical cult, in so far as it is new wine poured into old wineskins, that is, the supernatural activity of God poured into natural religious forms. The supernatural content of liturgy made Christianity different from the Judaism out of which it arose, even as it borrowed similar traits and cultic practices from both Judaism and Hellenism. "Only by understanding the eschatological and ecclesiological basis of this 'metamorphosis' can we properly understand what constitutes historically the innate antinomy of the Christian *lex orandi*: its unquestionable continuity with Jewish tradition and its equally unquestionable newness."[24] Schmemann thinks there is a reason why the Church adopted the word *leitourgia* in the first place, instead of using other sacred vocabulary that was available at the time. The selection of this word "indicates her special understanding of worship, which is indeed a revolutionary one. If Christian worship is *leitourgia*, it cannot be simply reduced to, or expressed in terms of, 'cult.' The ancient world knew a plethora of cultic religions or 'cults'. ... But the Christian cult is *leitourgia*, and this means that it is *functional* in its essence, has a goal to achieve which transcends the categories of cult as such."[25]

Christianity is not one religion among others, it is the Son of God incarnate, uniting himself to his mystical body through the Holy Spirit, as he himself is united to the Father (John 17). Although the *leitourgia* of the Church occurs in a form that looks like other religious cult (there are priests, temples, sacrifices, sacred Scriptures, etc.), it is actually an exercise of eschatology on earth. "Thus fasting and Eucharist form, so to say, two complementary and necessary poles of Church life, [and] manifest the essential antinomy of her nature: expectation and possession, fullness and growth, eschatology and history."[26] If this tension between eschatology and history is ever weakened, like the tension of a tightrope walker's cable is ever weakened, then the Church falls either into hope for utopia or a tendency to exercise power in this world. These are the two contradictory choices that Schmemann is trying to avoid. If the Orthodox are spared this struggle between utopian irrelevancy and political relevancy, it is "not because they have remained faithful to the eschatological antinomy of Christianity, but because of a gradual transformation of Orthodoxy either into a clerical ritual and magic religion, or into a spirituality which denies the world."[27]

This twin application of antinomy — the Christian being for the world and yet opposed to it, and the Christian cult being continuous with human worship and yet transcending it — is necessary background to understand Schmemann's idea of liturgy for the life of the world.

Commenting on a series of theological affirmations, he says that none of the errors denounced "would have been possible without, first of all, a dislocation and a breakdown of the transcendence-immanence antinomy itself, of the fundamental Christian *theologia...*"[28] Schmemann expends a good deal of effort trying to read the signs of the time. (Indeed, he characterizes one collection of essays as having been written "more often than not as an *ad hoc* response to, or reflection upon, some event, some development that I considered to be a vital significance for the Orthodox Church."[29]) The published Journals give us further insight into how this is processed in his mind. In one entry he reflects upon the fact that the followers of Hegel worshiped history, and now, at the next swing of the pendulum, a generation is dethroning history. Some say humanity can only find meaning by serving history, but others say humanity can only find meaning by being liberated from history. The tragedy of contemporary Christianity, says Schmemann, is that we have accepted this either-or. Failing the antinomous relationship of eschaton and history, Church and world, liturgy and the mundane, we lapse into *airesis*, and make our choice to either leave history or else settle into it as our home. Schmemann objects in a lengthy quote from the Journals.

"Ultimately the whole novelty of Christianity consisted (consists) in destroying this choice, this polarization. *This* is the essence of Christianity as Eschatology. The Kingdom of God is the goal of history, and the Kingdom of God is already now *among us, within us.* Christianity is a unique historical event, and Christianity is the presence of that event as the completion of all events and of history itself. ...

Here is, for me, *the whole meaning of liturgical theology.* The Liturgy: the joining, revelation, actualization of the historicity of Christianity (remembrance) and of its transcendence over that historicity.

Hence, the link of the Church with the world, the Church *for the world*, but as its beginning and its end, as the affirmation that the world is *for the Church*, since the Church is the presence of the kingdom of God.

Here is the eternal antinomy of Christianity and the essence of all contemporary discussions about Christianity. The task of theology is to be faithful to the antinomy, which disappears in the experience of the Church as *pascha:* a *continuous* (not only historical) passage of the world to the Kingdom. All the time one must leave the world and all the time one must remain it." [30]

Let us diagram that quote. First he said the essence of Christianity is to discover the antinomy that the kingdom of God is both the goal of history and is already now among us; second, that the whole meaning of liturgical theology was in the joining together of the historicity of Christianity and

Christianity's transcendence over that historicity; third, the relationship between Church and world is antinomous because the Church is for the world and the world is for the Church; and fourth, the task of theology is to be faithful to this antinomy. (In our next conversation I will present this in syllogistic form as the basis of liturgical theology.[31])

The Kingdom and the World Meet in Liturgy

Liturgy is an experience and expression of the fact that the Kingdom is the goal of history and yet the Kingdom is already among us and within us. "The Kingdom is yet *to come*, and the Church is not *of* this world. And yet this Kingdom to come is already present, and the Church is fulfilled *in* this world."[32] In other words, liturgy is an experience and expression of the Church. The goal of liturgy is "the *Church* as the manifestation and presence of the 'new *aeon*' of the Kingdom of God."[33] And "the Church is the presence and action of the Holy Spirit."[34]

And that new aeon is the refreshment and transfiguration of all of creation. The liturgy consecrates the world, not just the Church, not just Christians. Does liturgy make the world irrelevant to Christians? No. Is the liturgy concerned with the world? Yes. It is concerned with this world's passage to the next world, concerned with the transformation of this very world and not its replacement by another. That is the Church's service to the world – its *leitourgia*.

A *leitourgia* is the work of a few on behalf of the many, says Schmemann, and as the *leitourgia* of ancient Israel "was the corporate work of a chosen few to prepare the world for the coming of the Messiah" the *leitourgia* of the Church itself is "a calling to act in the world after the fashion of Christ, to bear testimony to him and his kingdom."[35] That's why the Church chose this word to describe herself in action, instead of one of the available words from the roster of cultic terminology: the Church's *leitourgia* is to be a sacrament of the Kingdom, an efficacious sign.

"In the early Church ... even the term *leitourgia* was not, as it is today, a mere synonym of *cult*. It was applied indeed to all those ministries and offices within the Church in which she manifested and fulfilled her nature and vocation; it had primarily ecclesiological and not cultic connotations."

Then how does *leitourgia* get connected with liturgy? Schmemann finishes the thought.

"And the very fact that subsequently it was identified especially with "Divine Liturgy," the central active Christian cult, reveals above all the peculiar character, the uniqueness of that cult itself, of its place and function within the Church. From the very beginning, this unique function was precisely to "make the Church what she is" – the witness and participant of the saving *event* of Christ, of the new life of the Holy Spirit, of the presence in "this world" of the kingdom to come."[36]

To express the antinomy one more time: the Church leaves the world but does not abandon it. The Eucharist is performed in time, not outside it, but what it reveals in time is something that time does not contain. This mystery has entered history in order to draw all of history toward itself. "The essence of the liturgy is in leaving the fallen, fragmented time and moving into a time restored in all its fullness. In that sense, the whole liturgy is in the Spirit."[37]

The Church is the presence of the Kingdom in time, and at the liturgy we experience the Church fulfilling herself. This is what and why Christians celebrate. They experience the Church as sacrament of the Kingdom, and though it is antinomically contained in cultic rites, it is not a religious cultic act. What is the Kingdom of God and how does one experience it now?

"To this question the early Church, at least, had an answer: to her the Kingdom of God was revealed and made "known" every time she gathered on the eighth day – the day of the *Kyrios* – "to eat and drink at Christ's table in His Kingdom," to proclaim His death and confess His resurrection, to immerse herself in the "new eon" of the Spirit. One can say that the uniqueness, the radical novelty of the new Christian *leitourgia* was here, in this "entrance" into the Kingdom which for "this world" is still "to come," but of which the Church is truly the sacrament: the beginning, the anticipation, and the "parousia." And the liturgy, especially the Eucharist, was precisely the *passage* of the Church from this world into heaven, the act by which and in which she fulfilled herself becoming "that which she is": entrance, ascension, communion. But, and this is the most important point, it was precisely this eschatological, i.e. Kingdom-centered and Kingdom-oriented character of the liturgy that made it – in the experience and the understanding of the early Church – the source of the

Church's evaluation of the world, the root and the motivation of her mission to the world. It is because Christians – in the *passage* and *ascension* to heaven – knew the Kingdom and partook of its "joy and peace in the Holy Spirit" that they could truly be its *witness* in and to the world."[38]

Experience of the eschatological liturgy does not alienate Christians from the world, it is the source of their motivation to undertake mission to the world.

The Liturgical Mission to the World

That mission has two phases. First a negative phase of liberation, and second a positive phase of ascension. So long as this world is under the dominion of Satan (and that will be the case until the final judgment) the first mission of the Church to the world is its emancipation. "It is liturgy which, by revealing to men the Kingdom, makes life and history, nature and matter a pilgrimage, an ascension towards the Kingdom. It is liturgy, in short, that is the power, given to the Church, to overcome and destroy all 'idols' — and secularism is one of them. But liturgy is all this only if we ourselves accept and use it as power."[39] We could call this exorcism, if we understood the term to mean reclaiming something for its original purpose. What was the original purpose of the cosmos? and of man and woman in it? Satan's lie must be exposed, and doing so reclaims a cosmos that has belonged to God from the beginning. The Eucharist is "the journey of the church into the dimension of the Kingdom. ... it is not an escape from the world, rather it is the arrival at a vantage point from which we can see more deeply into the reality of the world."[40]

Then can begin the second mission to the world, lifting it up. "Since the day of Pentecost there is a seal, a ray, a sign of the Holy Spirit on everything or those who believe in Christ and know that He is the life of the world – and that in Him the world in its totality has become again a *liturgy*, a *communion,* an *ascension.'*[41] The teleology of the cosmos is to become a liturgy; the teleology of man and woman is to be recovered liturgists, since sin in the garden of Eden was the abandonment of our liturgical career. The liturgy must now happen sacramentally, i.e., under signs and within the institutional Church, but it is not meant to remain there. By the ascetical and sacramental and authoritative and magisterial activity of the Church we are restored to our cosmic priesthood. Within the sacred liturgy we learn how to do the mundane liturgy. We are taught and empowered. We learn the telos of all things so that we know how to use them when we encounter them in our daily life. We are given back the operating instructions for matter and society and history and our own lives, which we misplaced in our hasty exit from the garden of Eden. Schmemann writes,

> "For in liturgical worship we are not only put "in contact" with God, but are given the vision of the Kingdom of God, as fulfillment in Him of all that exists, of all that He has created for Himself, and also

we are made partakers of that new Reality. And having seen and tasted of the "heaven and earth as full of His glory" we are then to relate all life, all activity, all time to this vision and experience, to judge and to transform our life by it."[42]

We must ascend to heaven in order to become partakers of the world to come, but the eschatological antinomy is that this world to come is already within us, waiting for us to transform our world in accordance with it. "It is the very essence of the Christian faith that we live in a kind of rhythm – leaving, abandoning, denying the world, and yet at the same time always returning to it; living in time by that which is beyond time; living by that which is not yet come, but which we already know and possess."[43]

I can conclude with an affirmation of three expressions of antinomy from Schmemann. First, liturgy is an antinomy of *withdrawal in order to draw closer*. "The fundamental liturgical experience of withdrawal from 'this world' is understood not in terms of a spiritualistic or apocalyptic 'escape,' but as the starting point, as indeed the foundation, of Christian mission in action in the world, for it is this experience that makes it possible to see the world in Christ."[44] Second, liturgy is an antinomy of *separation and reunion*: "We separate ourselves from the world in order to bring it, in order to lift it up to the kingdom, to make it once again the way to God and participation in his eternal kingdom."[45] Third, liturgy is an antinomy of a *useless rite becoming useful* to the world: "For the liturgy was always experienced and understood in our Church as precisely the entering of men into, and communion with, the reality of the Kingdom of God, as that experience of God which alone makes possible everything else – all 'action', all 'fight.' And in this sense the less pragmatic and 'world-oriented' it is – the more 'useful' it is."[46]

Should liturgy matter outside the Church? Yes. The world is the matter of liturgy: raw material for sacrament, the substance of our sacrificial oblation, the nature that grace is perfecting, the history that the eschaton is ripening, the arena for the liturgy after the liturgy, the province of the Church's *leitourgia*, the object of exorcism and blessing, place of soul and body that are being transfigured. The Church is "new life and redeems therefore the whole life, the total being of man. And this whole life of man is precisely the world in which and by which he lives."[47]

Chapter 2: Can Theology be Done outside the Academy? Schmemann's Concept of Theology

At the end of our previous conversation about Schmemann's concept of liturgy we came to a lengthy quote in which Schmemann made four affirmations. They were (a) the Kingdom of God is both the goal of history and is already now among us; (b) liturgical theology's whole meaning is the joining together of Christianity's historicity and transcendence; (c) the relationship between Church and world is antinomous, such that all the time one must leave the world and all the time one must remain it; and (c) theology should be faithful to this eschatological antinomy as celebrated in the liturgy. From that series of affirmations I suggest a syllogism that would bridge his concept of liturgy with his concept of theology:

(1) the task of theology is to be faithful to the antinomy

(2) this antinomy is experientially known in liturgy

(3) therefore liturgy is the ontological condition for

doing faithful theology

I would like to walk across that bridge now, but we can do so

by an easy way or by a hard way. I will choose the latter: let us

take the hard way across the bridge! But before we do, let us

pause to look at the alternative, the easy way of trying to

connect liturgy and theology.

The Easy Path Not Taken

Should we bring liturgy and theology nearer together?

Absolutely. Would it be a valuable accomplishment?

Absolutely. How is this usually pursued? Usually in one or the

other of two directions. On the one hand, someone might

nudge theology closer to liturgy. Someone might argue that

academic theology should take liturgy more seriously than it

does. From atop the ivory tower, the academic lighthouse

could train its spotlight of theology upon a hundred topics in

the landscape below, and argue that liturgy should be one

among them. I think this is what Robert Taft is suggesting when he says,

> "To think that a homily of John Chrysostom or John Calvin, or a book by Karl Rahner or Karl Barth, is worthy of the theologian's attention, and fail to understand how the ways and the prayers by which these same gentlemen along with some other millions have worshiped God is worthy of the same, is the prejudice of those so locked into a narrow concept of expression as to think that only words communicate anything theological. Christian faith is not a set of verbal propositions."[48]

Under this first option we could propose that liturgy is an object worthy of the attention of the academy because most Christians will bump up against the Christian faith not in textbooks (not even in catechetical textbooks), they will bump up against Christianity in their sacramental life. No one can deny that liturgy is a historically significant component of

Christianity, and academic theology has numerous skills of investigation that it can bring to bear: its talent for systematic clarity; the comparative study of liturgical families; scriptural studies of the roots of liturgy; the investigation of liturgy's historical development; applied linguistic analysis; the study of medieval sacramentaries; ethnographic religious studies; anthropological theories of ritual behavior; interdisciplinary studies with music, art, and architecture; cultural and social ritual behavior; technologies of self-formation and formation of communities; a hermeneutic for reading liturgical texts; and a hermeneutic by which to "read" body, position, gesture, and symbol. It is an easy argument to make that theology should be more open to studying liturgical topics.

On the other hand, and in the other direction, someone might nudge liturgy closer to the academy. Someone might treat liturgy as a type of existential belief on the part of the academic theologian. The scholar who is engaged in a study of Bible, dogma, Church history, ethics, etc. might, in addition, happen to personally believe the Gospel message and so be drawn to worship with the Christian community. He or she might be led out of the library and into the sanctuary once a week, to rub shoulders with pious believers, before each returns to their regular corner: the laity to the world where they conduct their business, and the scholars to the university office where they conduct theirs. Of course, we can find some academics who assert this is not necessary, and will claim they can do their work without any personal belief, as I once heard a professor at the American Academy of Religion say. "I do not have to do what they do in order to study it; I do not have to believe what they believe in order to analyze it. Indeed, I have a better and more objective viewpoint because I don't do it or believe it." He supposed that this is how theological objectivity is achieved. But with a little nudging, we might bring liturgical practice within the orbit of theological rumination. A matchmaker would arrange for their marriage through some shared interest in sacramentology, or history, or architecture, or the arts.

There are other easy solutions we might strategize, but I'll stop here because they would all be variations upon either making theology more relevant to the Church, or making liturgy more relevant to the academy. Schmemann will also, occasionally, speak this way.

"It is indeed our first duty to acknowledge that for centuries theology was alienated from the Church and that this alienation had tragic consequences for both theology and the Church. ... [Theology] today constitutes within the Church a self-centered world, virtually isolated from the Church's life. It lives in itself and by itself in tranquil academic quarters, well defended against profane intrusions and curiosities by a highly technical language. Theologians avoid discussing the trivial reality of the Church's life, and do not even dream about influencing it in any way. In turn the Church, i.e., the bishops, priests and laity, are supremely indifferent to the writings of the theologians, even when they do not regard them with open suspicion. ... Theology simply fails to reach anybody but professionals, to provoke anything but esoteric controversies in academic periodicals."[49]

In such a quote, Schmemann is talking about theologians as we normally talk about theologians – the people with jobs in the academy who are paid to talk about other people who talk about God. So he concludes, "No wonder, therefore, that deprived of interest on the part of the Church, squeezed into the narrow limits of a professional clerical school, theology is guided in its inner life not by the experience, needs or problems of the Church but by individual interests of individual theologians."[50] It is an easy argument to make that there should be traffic back a nd forth across the bridge, since the Church needs theology, and theology should pay attention to the liturgical celebrations of the Church.

The Harder Path We Will Take

But our question – the question I want to ask in this second session – is whether theology can be done outside the academy. The easy attempt we have just witnessed answers: "No, it cannot, because theology is an academic skill set. Theology is located down the hall from the sociology office, the psychology office, the history and philosophy offices. No matter how seriously the theologian treats liturgy, the academy is where theology dwells, and the place where it is done. Either liturgy must be imported or theology must be exported." A harder path presents itself, however, if we adopt a different starting point, and I propose this is Schmemann's starting point. He asks the harder question: Is liturgy an *object* of theology, or is liturgy the *source* of theological thinking? It is true that if liturgy is an object for study, then we must either roll liturgy across the bridge into the courtyard of the academy, or lead a field trip out of the ivory tower to examine liturgy. But what if liturgy is not an object, but a source? He proposes we follow the Church Fathers' approach. "Just as they do not theologize about the Church, the Fathers do not theologize about the liturgy. Liturgy as the life, as the 'sacrament' of the Church is not the 'object' but the source of their theology because it is the epiphany of the Truth, of that fullness from which the 'mouth speaks.'"[51]

Kavanagh was able to further sharpen this question by introducing his famous "Mrs. Murphy." She has been criticized from various perspectives, and for various reasons. Even Kavanagh's good friend, Robert Taft, sounds a note of caution.

"In my view, the contemporary *theologia prima/theologia secunda* or primary/secondary theology debate seems to have the academy unduly agitated largely because we have not yet succeeded in burying Aidan Kavanagh's redoubtable Mrs Murphy. Part of the problem must, I think, be laid squarely at Aidan's feet. Aidan had a way with words, but he sometimes got entangled in the cuteness of his own rhetoric. His legendary Mme. Murphy is a classic instance of this. Unable to leave well-enough alone once he had created her, Aidan continued to wax eloquent on her as a "primary theologian" thereby muddying the waters and sidetracking the whole debate."[52]

Despite my respect for Taft, and the fact that his brainpower outweighs mine tenfold, and his knowledge exceeds mine a hundredfold, I respectfully disagree. Mrs. Murphy does *not* muddy the waters, she clarifies them, because she forces the question that needs to be asked: Can we use the name "theologian" for someone who does not treat the liturgy as an *object* but as a *source*? Mrs. Murphy's presence in the room forces the question upon us.

Schmemann is misunderstood by many to desire the reduction of theology to liturgy, as if "liturgical theology" would be produced by restricting theology to the study of liturgy. But Schmemann protests that this is an unfair characterization of his intention. This kind of reduction has appeared

> "only as a result of the unhealthy mutual alienation between theology and liturgy, and is therefore a kind of illegitimate child of an illegitimate situation. All theology, indeed, ought to be "liturgical," yet not in the sense of having liturgy as its unique "object" of study, but in that of having its ultimate term of reference in the faith of the Church, as manifested and communicated in the liturgy; that catholic vision and experience which it now lacks in its alienation from liturgy."[53]

To say that all theology should be Eucharistic does not mean that the Eucharist is the only thing theology speaks about. To say that all theology ought to be liturgical does not mean that the liturgy is the only object that theology looks at. Schmemann is not proposing that we reduce theology's range to nothing but liturgical topics, he rather proposes the rooting of theology in the liturgical experience. The liturgical movement brought some advance towards this end, but Schmemann thinks there was also ambiguity to be found there, and he offers two different names to the two different options that came out of it.

> "One speaks, for example, of liturgical theology, of a liturgical "ressourcement" of theology. For some, this implies an almost radical rethinking of the very concept of theology, a complete change in its structure. The *leitourgia* – being the unique expression of the Church, of its faith and of its life – must become the basic source of theological thinking, a kind of *locus theologicus par excellence*. There are those, on the other hand, who, while admitting the importance of the liturgical experience for theology, would rather consider it as a necessary object of theology – an object requiring, first of all, a theological clarification of its nature and function. Liturgical theology or the

theology of liturgy – we have here two entirely different views concerning the relationship between worship and theology."[54]

It should be clear that he prefers the name – and method – of the first group.

The contrast between the two is sharp, even diametrical. Schmemann repeatedly distinguishes between them, and I offer only three examples. First, he writes, "It is the 'discovery' of this distinction between theology of the liturgy and liturgical theology which stands, in my opinion, as the principal attainment of the liturgical movement."[55] Second, he writes that when we turn to the liturgy itself "what we discover then is the genuine liturgical theology, and this means that theology for which liturgy is not an 'object,' but its very source. We discover, in other terms, the forgotten truths of the ancient saying: *lex orandi est lex credendi.*"[56] And third, he explains what is wrong with the "theology of liturgy" approach.

"I designate by "theology of the liturgy" all study of the Church's cult in which this cult is analyzed, understood and defined in its "essence" as well as in its "forms" with the help of and in terms of theological categories and concepts which are exterior to the cult itself, that is, to its liturgical *specificity*. In this case, in other words, the liturgy is "subordinated" to, if not subject to, theology because it receives from theology its "meaning" as well as the definition of its place and function within the church. ... It is to this state of affairs (is it necessary to remind anyone?) that the liturgy has fallen since the appearance of that theology known as "systematic," which sets itself over against the idea of *liturgical theology*. Liturgical theology, on the other hand, is based upon the recognition that the liturgy in its totality is not only an "object" of theology, but above all its *source*, and this by virtue of the liturgy's essential ecclesial function: i.e., that of revealing by the means which are proper to it (and which belong only to it) the faith of the Church; in other words, of being that *lex orandi* in which the *lex credendi* finds its principal criterion and standard."[57]

Liturgy does not receive from theology its meaning, definition, place, and function within the Church. Instead liturgy, in addition to being a potential object of study, is above all the source of theology. If this is so, then theology is born when the Church gathers at Eucharist, and those who live from this source receive wisdom by which to understand the true objects of theology. Mrs. Murphy has the charismatic gift of theology.

"[In] the life of the Church the Eucharist is the moment of truth which makes it possible to see the real "objects" of theology: God, man and the world, in the true light, which, in other words, reveals both the objects of theology as they really are and gives the necessary light for their understanding. "We have seen the true light, we have received the Heavenly Spirit ..." Theology, like any other Christian service or "*leitourgia*," is a charisma, a gift of the Holy Spirit. This gift is given in the Church, i.e., in the act in which the Church fulfills herself as the communion of the Holy Spirit, in which she offers in Christ and offers Him, and is accepted by Christ and receives from Him; in the act which is, therefore, the source of all charisms and ministries of the Church."[58]

There are several crucial claims in this quote. First, this understanding of liturgical theology does not approach liturgy as an object of contemplation; second, theology concerns God, and God's revelation is epiphanized in the liturgy; and third, theology is a charismatic gift of the Holy Spirit given in the Church, given to the Church, given so that the Church may fulfill her *leitourgia*. Liturgy is a mission. The *leitourgia* of Israel was the work of a few to prepare the world for the coming of the Messiah; the *leitourgia* of the New Israel is a charisma of communion preparing humanity for eschatological communion at the heavenly banquet. This preparation is theology in action; this *leitourgia* is the source of theology.

Liturgy as Ontological Condition for Theology

It would be an easy compromise to say that theology occurs both in liturgy and in the academy, but as I've insisted, Schmemann is going further than that. He is not arguing that we accept liturgy as a tagalong, second rate, additional site for doing theology, he is proposing liturgy as the ontological condition for theology. Theology is made possible by participation in *leitourgia*.

> "The formula *lex orandi est lex credendi* means nothing else than that theology is *possible* only within the Church, i.e. as a fruit of this new life in Christ, granted in the sacramental *leitourgia*, as a witness to the eschatological fullness of the Church, as in other terms, a participation in this *leitourgia*. The problem of

the relationship between liturgy and theology is not for the Fathers a problem of priority or authority. Liturgical tradition is not an "authority" or a *locus theologicus*; it is the ontological condition of theology, of the proper understanding of kerygma, of the Word of God, because it is in the Church, of which the *leitourgia* is the expression and the life, that the sources of theology are functioning as precisely "sources.""[59]

When theology fails to operate from out of the place where sources function as sources, then it drifts to its own corner, while liturgy drifts to its corner, both apparently independent and autonomous activities, neither having anything to do with the other. This way of thinking created a crisis that assumed different forms in East and West.

In his own Eastern Orthodox Church, Schmemann says that the liturgical tradition "has played practically no role, and has been almost totally ignored, even as a *locus theologicus*. Liturgy and theology have peacefully coexisted – the former in its traditional form, the latter as the sacred science…"[60] In

the Western tradition he does not find a peaceful coexistence,

rather he finds theology aggressively imposing itself upon

liturgy, a first time when medieval scholasticism impacted the

very forms of liturgical life, and a second time when the

reformers replaced this with their own theology of worship.

In the story of the West, "Theology not only remained

internally independent of worship, but claimed the right to

control it, and to form it according to the *lex credendi*."[61] Such

lex credendi, it need not be said, came from the minds of

private theologians, instead of from the mind of the Church,

and exercised a kind of monopoly by theology over liturgy.

This resulted in a double crisis, affecting both theology and

liturgy, because a crisis is always a divorce: life drifts away

from its own foundations. Addressing that crisis must "shape

our agenda, if theology is for us more than a quiet 'academic'

activity; if we understand it as our specific charism and

ministry within the Body of Christ."[62] Schmemann can give a foreboding description of what will happen to theology, indeed, what has happened to theology, if the connection to liturgy is sundered.

> "I am saying this out of a very deep conviction – something has happened to theology itself in the history of the Church. It was disconnected from its living source, from the only living source, and that is the liturgy. ... Theology became a void, a mere intellectual status in the Church without any real reference to the liturgy. ... What also happened was that theology became a professional occupation for theologians. ... Theology did not care about the liturgy, and the liturgy did not care about theology. There was a real divorce. ... My point is that theology remained an intellectual preoccupation. It was cut off from the living source which makes it not only an adequate expression of the Church's truth, but something more than that, a real and living testimony

to the life and spirit of the Church. ... The time has come for putting those two realities back where they belong together. The liturgy is to become again the source of theology."[63]

The idea of theology being a charismatic *leitourgia* instead of a quiet academic activity is so foreign to our ordinary understanding that we scarcely know how to talk about it. We find it equally difficult to speak of a theologian possessing a charismatic mission. Yet, in his memoriam to Vladimir Lossky Schmemann says "Orthodox theology has lost one of its most gifted and devoted servants, one of those for whom theology is a unique and sacred 'charisma' in the Church, requiring the sacrifice of their whole life."[64]

Can theology be done outside the academy? Yes. It is done every eighth day, in the midst of the community assembled at the altar of the Lord, under inspiration of the Holy Spirit, infused with the life of Christ, ascending to the Father. Theology is an experience of eschaton suffusing the temporal, our response to the new Adam, the new age, the new aeon. Theology is born from liturgy. "Theology is always an invitation 'to taste and see,'" Schmemann says, "an announcement and a promise to be fulfilled in communion, vision and life."[65] The Holy Fathers of the Church knew this because they included in their understanding of theology what the modern scholar dismissively calls "practical and pastoral." In other words, the eternal salvation of man was their total attention.

> "Words and ideas were for them directly related not simply to Truth and Error, but to the Truth that *saves* and to the error that brings with it death and damnation. And it is their constant, truly "existential" preoccupation with, and their total commitment to, salvation of real, concrete men that makes every line they wrote so ultimately serious and their theology so vital and so precisely pastoral. Intellectual as it is, their theology is always addressed not to "intellectuals,"

but to the whole Church, in the firm belief that everyone in the Church has received the Spirit of Truth and was made a "theologian" – i.e., a man concerned with God."[66]

Everyone in the Church was made a theologian, if theologian means someone concerned with God. Mrs. Murphy is brought by the third person of the Trinity, through the second person of the Trinity, into communion with the first person of the Trinity. So Tomas Spidlik defines theology in the context of the Trinity. "The ancient Christian East understood the practice of theology only as a personal communion with *Theos*, the Father, through the *Logos*, Christ, in the Holy Spirit – an experience lived in a state of prayer."[67] And Archimandrite Vasileos defines theology as life. "True theology is always living, a form of hierurgy, something that changes our life and 'assumes' us into itself: we are to become theology. Understood in this way, theology is not a matter for specialists but a universal vocation; each is called to become a "theologian soul."[68] Can theology be done outside the academy? Yes. It should be done in our souls.

Remember our syllogism: (i) theology is faithfulness to the antinomy of the new age already dawning in this present age, (ii) and this antinomy is first known experientially in liturgy (and afterwards theoretically), (iii) therefore liturgy is the ontological condition for doing faithful theology. The Church is this new age dawning; theology is sourced in that nature of the Church; the Church-at-liturgy gives birth to theology; at liturgy we con-spire – breathe together – with the Holy Spirit; theology speaks by the eschatological air the Holy Spirit breathes into the Church; theology is spiritual language; what founds the Church and gives her life is not mere assent to a doctrine, it is a living relationship to the Paschal Mystery. The life, death, resurrection, glorification of Jesus, and the descent of the Holy Spirit on the day of Pentecost continue mystically in the Church's liturgy. Perpetuating the Paschal Mystery is the Church's *leitourgia*, i.e. her mission.

"[None] of these events can be known, in the rational meaning of that word, nor even believed in outside the experience which reveals their reality and makes us "witness to these things." But then theology cannot be anything else but the "description" of that experience, its revelation in human words and concepts. The Church is not an institution that keeps certain divinely revealed "doctrines" and "teachings" about this or that event of the past, but the very epiphany of these events themselves. And she can teach about them because, first of all, she knows them; because she is the experience of their reality. Her faith as teaching and theology is rooted in her faith as experience. Her *lex credendi* is revealed in her life."[69]

The Church is the experience of the reality of these events; these events, experienced, is the source of theology; secondary theology is the description of the mystery in action.

That is what it means to call liturgy a source, and not make it an object. The second order theologian knows a specialized jargon that permits him to examine the Church's description, if he is faithful to the tradition. But the first order theologian, like Mrs. Murphy, will describe her experience in her own, primary way. She has stepped into the new life that liturgy generates and communicates. She has experienced the life of the Church (*lex orandi*) and so knows, in non-specialized jargon, the *lex credendi* by which she and every Christian lives. She is a witness, and that is what makes her a theologian: she is an eyewitness of the eschatological antinomy. Schmemann writes, "It is this experience – radically new because it is not of 'this world,' but whose gift and presence, continuity and fulfillment in 'this world' is the Church – that for the Fathers constitutes the self-evident source of theology, the source of its very possibility as precisely *theology*, i.e. words adequate to God and adequate therefore to all reality."[70]

Theology is not an accomplishment, it is a gift. Theology is not a cogitation, it is a vision. Theology is not an achievement at the end of the University curriculum, it is sharing the vision of the Holy Spirit, which is also the experience of the Church. One approach to theology will fail to understand that, another approach will be founded upon it.

"A certain approach to theology, although of course it does not negate that experience, denies it the status of a "source" of theology, that of a *locus theologicus*. It draws a line between theology as a rational structure, as a science, and "mysticism," and it relegates the latter to a special religious category or phenomenon, distinct from theology. But in the Eastern Tradition all genuine theology is, of necessity and by definition, *mystical*. This means not that theology is at the mercy of individual and irrational "visions" and "experiences," but that it is rooted in, and made indeed *possible*, by the Church's experience of herself

as *communion of the Holy Spirit.*"[71]

The foundation of theology, the root which feeds it, is not our cleverness. This is what is wrong with scholasticism, according to the Orthodox. Scholasticism is their name for theology disconnected from the Church's self-experience as communion of the Holy Spirit. Schmemann writes, "It is indeed the 'original sin' of the entire western theological development that it made 'texts' the only *loci theologici*, the extrinsic 'authorities' of theology, disconnecting theology from its living source: liturgy and spirituality."[72] The tradition of sacraments and sacred rites is an inviolable element of Tradition, he says, and therefore one of the *sources* which theology must utilize. "The neglect of this source in scholastic theology is explained by a narrowing down of the concepts both of Tradition and of the Church. But the early Church firmly confessed the principle *lex orandi lex est credendi.*"[73] Schmemann does not object to theology being organized, systematic, ordered; and he acknowledges that there must be a crowning synthesis, which dogmatics can provide. Both Holy Tradition and Scripture are sources of dogmatics, but

"in order to use them properly, dogmatics must accept the evidence of Scripture and Tradition not in the form of "texts," but in the fullness and interrelatedness of their theological significance. Thus, between Scripture as a "text" and its use in dogmatics there stands biblical theology, and between worship as a fact and its use in dogmatics there stands liturgical theology."[74]

Although scholasticism is associated with the medieval west, Schmemann is using the term to identify an approach, a theological structure, that can also be found in the Orthodox east.

"By "scholastic" we mean, in this instance, not a definite school or period in the history of theology, but a theological structure which existed in various forms in both the West and the East, and in which all "organic" connection with worship is severed. Theology here has an independent, rational status; it is a search for a system of consistent categories and concepts: *intellectus fidei.* The position of worship in relation to theology is reversed: from a *source* it becomes an *object*, which has to be defined and evaluated within the accepted categories (e.g. definitions of sacraments). Liturgy supplies theology with "data," but the method of dealing with these data is independent of any liturgical context."[75]

If theology is not done in connection to its source, then it becomes an island of isolated scholasticism, severed from its wellspring.

A Conversion Required

I shall use this distinction to my advantage. Scholasticism and theology are distinguishable, and if so, we can agree that Mrs. Murphy is not a scholastic because she does not have the secondary academic skill required to examine worship as an object, yet we can claim Mrs. Murphy is a theologian because she is close to the source. The river of liturgy runs through her heart and mind, making her capable of theology, albeit in a different and primary way.[76] It turns out that Schmemann is not only talking about a conversion required by the whole system of theology, he is talking about a conversion of the theologian. Theology, he said, is an invitation to taste and see; theology is an act of witnessing and participating in the mystery itself.

"All this, however, requires not only a 'conversion' of theology itself, of its structure and methods, but, first of all, of the theologian. He has mastered to perfection the necessary asceticism of intellectual discipline and integrity, the humility proper to all genuine rational effort. He now has to learn how to immerse himself into the joy of the Church. ... He has to rediscover the oldest of all languages of the

Church: that of her rites, the rhythm in the *ordo* of her *leitourgia* in which she concealed from the eyes of "this world" her most precious treasure . ... He has to become again not only the student of the Church's faith but, above all, its *witness*."[77]

In this, the theologian turns out to be the scholastic's instructor. *Theologia prima* guides *theologia secunda* because the primary theologian is witness to the Paschal Mystery from within, where he or she learns the oldest of all the languages of the Church. Schmemann writes about this in his Journal.

"Pascha. Holy Week. Essentially, bright days such as are needed. And truly that is all that is needed. I am convinced that if people would really hear Holy Week, Pascha, the Resurrection, Pentecost, the Dormition, there would be no need for theology. All of theology is there. All that is needed for one's spirit, heart, mind and soul. How could people spend centuries discussing justification and redemption? It's all in these services. Not only is it revealed, it simply flows in one's heart and mind."[78]

All that theology would talk about can be seen in the purifying fire of the new age setting this world alight. The eschaton creeps stealthily forward to renew us because we become what we see, and we see Christ in his sacramental and ecclesial body. Schmemann asks himself what is absolute in Orthodoxy, and answers himself "I always come to the same conclusion: it is first of all a certain *vision*, an experience of God, the world, the man. The best in Orthodox theology is about that vision …"[79]

What we are talking about here is the experience of the Church at liturgy, like the experience of family is at the dining table, or at the ritual of the bedtime story. When we say the liturgy is the source, not object, of theology, we are saying that our own personal experiences or thoughts are not the basis of theology. We are to think with the mind of the Church. We conform ourselves to the Church's *lex orandi*, we

do not conform the Church's *lex credendi* to ourselves. It is
thinking within the context of "ecclesiality," a term Pavel
Florensky used to name how human beings experience truth
in its liturgical, mystical, and dogmatic dimensions.
Ecclesiality is the new life in the Spirit; it is the beauty of new
life in Absolute Beauty, understood as order and wholeness,
and it is one with Truth and Goodness.[80] This is Tradition as
the normative and apostolic experience of the risen Christ in
the Spirit. Theology is not thinking with an earthly mind
about heavenly subjects, it is thinking in communion with the
mind of Christ about all subjects, earthly and heavenly.[81] It is
true that theology uses words, but that does not mean that
theology only communicates concepts. What is
communicated theologically is this experience celebrated,
enacted, epiphanized, feasted upon by the Church. Again, in
his Journals, Schmemann writes:

> "I strongly feel that theology is the transmission in
> words – not of other words and beliefs, but of the

experience of the living Church, revealed now, communicated now. The theology that is being taught has estranged itself from the Church and from that experience; it has become self-sufficient and wants above all to be a science. Science about God, about Christ, about eternal life; therefore it has become unnecessary chatter."[82]

The *lex orandi* is the Paschal Mystery glowing in the liturgical rites, communicated to our hearts when the Holy Spirit creates in us a capacity of spiritual sight.

To "translate" is to lay something down in a new location: when the martyrs' bones were moved it was called the translation of relics. Before we translate liturgical event into language, the reality must be translated from heaven to earth so that it can be experienced. Liturgy is that translation of eschatological reality into our present life – the antinomy about which Schmemann speaks so often – and this is the very life of the Church. "The Church, in other terms, is not an 'essence' or 'being' distinct, as such, from God, man, and the world, but is the very reality of *Christ in us* and *us in Christ*, a new mode of God's presence and action in His creation, of creation's life in God."[83] The true form of the Church would be one in which that presence of Christ is celebrated, namely, the Eucharist: "the sacrament in which the Church performs the passage, the Passover, from this world into the Kingdom, offers in Christ the whole creation to God ... and partakes of Christ immortal life at His table in His Kingdom."[84]

When Schmemann talks about the liturgy being an expression of the Church's faith, he is talking about the Church being the new mode of Christ's presence and action in the cosmos. From his earliest book, and throughout his other writings, he has tried to say that "the 'essence' of the liturgy or *lex orandi* is ultimately nothing else but the Church's faith itself or, better to say, the manifestation, communication and fulfillment of that faith. It is in this sense that one must understand, it seems to me, the famous dictum *lex orandi est lex credendi.*"[85] If liturgical theology seeks to discover the theological meaning behind the liturgical facts,[86] it is only because the *lex credendi* is embodied in, expressed in, instantiated in, and rises from the *lex orandi.*

Restoring liturgy to its place as a source of theology will be crucial for what Schmemann calls a theological regeneration. In my closing quotation, drawn from across three paragraphs, Schmemann describes what has happened and what will happen to theology if this does not occur. Liturgical theology is not about rescuing liturgy from neglect by the academy. Liturgical theology has more to do with the regeneration of theology itself. Nudging liturgy closer to theology, or theology closer to liturgy does no harm; Schmemann admits that he has contributed to the process itself. But it is not enough.

"What do I mean when I speak about this reunion or reconnecting together again of the liturgy and the theology? I mean not only that it is an invitation to theologians to pay more attention to liturgical data .

... I was only trying to point out that the theologian

ought to be more liturgical and the liturgiologist must

be more theological. This would do no harm. I am

trying to go further than that and state, at least as my

conviction, that in a very direct and real way, not only

in a symbolical or educational way, but in a real way,

the Eucharist, the sacraments, and the liturgy of the

Church are the real sources of theology.

Now what do I mean? I mean that theology in

the Church is a charisma, a gift of the Holy Spirit, not

only a system of syllogisms and deductions, but a real

power to bear testimony toward God's doing in the

Church for the salvation of man. ... Where is that gift

of the Holy Spirit given? Where does theology find its

real and divine status if not in that sacrament of all

sacraments in which the Church eternally becomes

what she is, the temple of the Holy Spirit, the body of

Christ, the eschaton, the anticipation of the world to come? ... This is where the foundation of theology as a phenomenon *bene fundatum* is."[87]

To shuffle the words in the title of this talk: where can we find theology being done? Where is that gift of the Holy Spirit given? Where does theology find its real and divine status? Where is the foundation of theology? These are the questions Schmemann answers when he says liturgy is the ontological condition for theology.

Chapter 3: Do We Need Liturgy in Our Life? Schmemann's Connection between Liturgy and Spirituality

Last time we heard Schmemann define theology as a vision, and I think he meant a vision of *leitourgia*, not liturgy; a vision of Church, not cult; a vision of *mysterion*, not ceremony; a vision of a living world, not a dead one. In an essay titled "Prayer, Liturgy, and Renewal," Schmemann defines each of the terms I have selected. Regarding theology, he says that if renewal is to have "a consistent orientation and this means precisely a *theology*, this theology must be rooted, first of all, in the recovered Christian *eschatology*."[88] Regarding *leitourgia*, he says it is "a corporate procession and passage of the Church toward her fulfillment, the sacrament of the Kingdom of God."[89] Regarding the Church, he concludes that "she exists not for herself but for the world and its salvation."[90] Regarding the *mysterion,* he says it was reclaimed when the liturgical movement recovered the paschal dimension of the liturgy. "The most important aspect of the Movement ... is that this 'rediscovery' of Pascha was not a simple return to the past, not 'archaeology' and 'antiquity,' but the spring of a truly new vision of the Church and of her mission in the world."[91] And what about the world? What about the arena that we are asking whether liturgy should enter?

"What is the "world" of which one speaks so much today? ... We seem to forget that in the New Testament and in the whole Christian tradition the "world" is the object of two apparently contradicting attitudes: an emphatic acceptance, a *yes*, but also an equally emphatic rejection, a *no*. [He references John 3:16 about saving the world, and John 2:15 about not loving the world.] ... The whole point precisely is that the New Testament and the Christian tradition allow no choice and no reduction. They accept and reject the world simultaneously ..."[92]

The world is intended to be the "sacrament of the kingdom,"[93] he adds, but fallen humanity fails to take it that way, thereby wounding the world, as Paul describes in Romans 8. Do we need liturgy in our life? Yes, if we are to do the world as it was meant to be done. This is the context of liturgical spirituality.

Schmemann says that the Church experiences the Kingdom of God in the *mysterion* of her liturgy, which celebrates the Kingdom's transformation of all creation. This brings about new life and redeems the total being of humanity. "And this whole life of man is precisely the world in which and by which he lives. … One can say that 'this world' is saved and redeemed every time a man responds to the divine gift, accepts it and lives by it."[94] But when our understanding of eschatology began to change then our understanding of the Kingdom began to change. When theologians began treating the Kingdom as one of the "last things," it made the work of the Kingdom seem like the arrival of another world, a replacement and not a renewal.

Loss of this eschatological capacity has affected East and West differently, but it has affected them both.

> "In my own tradition, the Byzantine, this has meant, for example, the appearance of endless symbolic explanations of worship, and so the eucharistic Liturgy that is the heart of the Church has been transformed in effect into a series of audio-visual aids. ... In the West, on the other hand, once the eschatological dimension of the sacraments was forgotten, there developed a constant emphasis upon the notion of the Real Presence . ... the West obscured its true meaning by making a sharp distinction between symbol and reality; ..."[95]

This faulty understanding of eschatology resulted in "a shift and also a 'split' in Christian piety. There were, on the one hand, those who for the sake of the soul and its salvation not only rejected but also ignored the world ...; on the other hand, there were those who for the sake of the world began to ignore more and more, if not to reject, the 'other world.'"[96] Will liturgy accompany us into the world? Some say no, and believe we should discard the world and turn to the business of saving souls; some others say no, and believe we should discard liturgical matters and turn to the business of improving the world. You see that these are flip sides of the same mistake, famously described as the "spiritualist" and "activist" in the first chapter of *For the Life of the World*. Will the liturgy accompany us into the world? I think Schmemann says yes, and this is what he means by "liturgical piety."

Schmemann has set out to rescue the eschatological dimension of liturgy so that the antinomy of Kingdom and world can be restored. The *leitourgia*, he says, is an epiphany of the Church's eschatological identity, the entrance into the Kingdom; the Church, he says, is the presence of the Kingdom of God, for she is truly the sacrament of the Kingdom; and the *mysterion*, he says, is "the holding-together, in a mystical and existential, rather than rational, synthesis of both the total *transcendence* of God and his genuine *presence*. But this mystery is precisely that of the Kingdom of God, the faith and the piety of the Church being rooted in the experience *now* of that which is to come... ."[97] The faith and piety of the Church must be rooted in the present liturgical experience of something that is being unfolded from out of God's deep will, and since we experience the Kingdom-to-come in the liturgy, liturgy is the source of the Church's piety. Liturgy is the root; piety is the stalk, flower, and fruit that grows from it, for the sake of the world.

In order to explore this, I propose that we must deal with three facets of Schmemann's thought. First, we must identify what he thinks liturgical piety does *not* mean. Second, that will allow us to identify what he thinks liturgical piety *does* mean. And third, we shall be in a position appreciate what he means when he describes man and woman being cosmic priests.

What Liturgical Piety is Not

First, then, what is the idea of liturgical piety that Schmemann *rejects*? It can be found in an interpretation that many people have given to the liturgical movement. "It is true that many still do not understand the real nature of the liturgical movement. Everything is still fettered by the categories of 'school theology.' It is thought that this is nothing more than a new awakening of an aesthetically religious, psychological enthusiasm for cultus, for its ceremonial and ritual, for its external aspects; a sort of new liturgical pietism."[98] I suppose it is an easy linguistic mistake to make: "liturgical piety" is translated as "piety for the liturgy." We confuse the relationship between the adjective and the noun: liturgical piety is thought to be an increased infatuation with the liturgy. But this self-absorbed attitude is *not* what Schmemann intends, and it wearies him so much that he creates a name for it. "I realize how spiritually tired I am of all this 'Orthodoxism,' of all the fuss with Byzantium,

Russia, way of life, spirituality, church affairs, piety, of all these rattles. I do not like any one of them, and the more I think about the meaning of Christianity, the more it all seems alien to me. It all literally obscures Christ, pushes Him into the background."[99] Here are two other names for it. "There is nothing more alien to the true spirit of Orthodox liturgy than a certain superstitious 'liturgiologism', or an 'eschatologism' which reduces the whole Christian life to communion and despises everything else as 'vain.'"[100] And here is a final word for it: "Does this contemporary Orthodox 'liturgism' constitute a happy state of affairs? Does it correspond to the church's everlasting 'rule of prayer'? Is it a realization of that 'worship' in Spirit and in Truth' which was given to the Church by the commandment of Christ?" [101]

How did this happen? Through a trifurcation of what should have been a three-way unity. Such sundering is precisely what he characterizes as "Western" and "scholastic."

"For it is clear that this deeply "Westernized" theology has had a very serious impact on worship, or rather, on the experience and comprehension of worship, on that which elsewhere I have defined as liturgical piety. And it has had this impact because it satisfied a deep desire of man for a legalistic religion that would fulfill his need for both the "sacred" – a divine sanction and guarantee – and the "profane," i.e., a natural and secular life protected, as it were, from the constant challenge and absolute demands of God. ... And yet this is exactly what happened to our "liturgical piety" ..."[102]

Yes, liturgical piety can be defined as the experience and comprehension of worship, but not if that worship isolates God from our daily life in the hope that he will not bother us there. The risk of this faulty understanding of liturgical piety is the production of a legalistic religion that protects us from God's demands on every facet of our life. *Pietas* means devotion or dutiful conduct, but in this mistaken view we believe we can expend our duty to God by fiddling with the liturgy. No residual devotion would be required of us outside the temple.

Schmemann insists that the Church's *leitourgia* has broader implications. The reason liturgical piety fell into a deficient form was because theology fell into a deficient understanding of *leitourgia*; i.e., theologians began circumscribing *leitourgia* to cult.

"If Christian worship is *leitourgia,* it cannot be simply reduced to, or expressed in terms of "cult." The ancient world knew a plethora of cultic religions or "cults" – in which worship or cultic acts were the only real content of religion, an "end in itself." But the Christian cult is *leitourgia* and this means that it is *functional* in its essence, has a goal to achieve which transcends the categories of cult as such. This goal is precisely the *Church* as the manifestation and presence of the "new eon," of the Kingdom of God. In a sense the Church is indeed a *liturgical institution*, i.e. an institution whose *leitourgia* is to fulfill itself as the Body of Christ and a new creation. Christian cult is, therefore, a radically new cult, unprecedented in both the Old Testament and paganism, and the deficiency of a certain theology, as well as of a certain liturgical piety, is that they not only overlook the radical newness of Christian *leitourgia* but rather define and experience it again in the old cultic categories."[103]

Leitourgia transcends the categories of cult because its true purpose is to produce the Church as a sacramental manifestation of the new age, embedded in the world with the ministry of bringing life to the world. Unfortunately, with the reduction of *leitourgia* to cult came a concomitant reduction of piety's range of concern. There arose a "non-ecclesiological and non-eschatological orientation of liturgical piety. If the liturgy remained very much the heart and the center of the Church's life, if in some ways it became its almost unique expression, it was no longer comprehended as the act which 'existentially' refers us to the three inseparable realities of the Christian faith: the world, the Church, the Kingdom."[104]

Getting past this mindset is not easy. When we speak of liturgical piety, we must come to understand that the Church-at-liturgy is not a matter of entering further into cult, it is a matter of already living eschatologically, and drawing the world into this life, too. Such eschatology is not to be interpreted as an escape from the world. On the contrary, it is

> "the very source and foundation of the Christian doctrine of the world and of the Church's action in the world. By referring the world[,] every moment of its time, every ounce of its matter and all human thought, energy, and creativity to the "eschaton," to the ultimate reality of the Kingdom of God, it gives them their only real meaning, their proper

"entelechy." Thus, it makes possible Christian action as well as the judgment and evaluation of that action. Yet the "locus" of that recovery is the liturgy of the Church. For eschatology is not a "doctrine," an intellectual construction ... but a dimension of all faith and of all theology. ... And the proper function of the Christian *leitourgia*, as I have tried to show, is precisely to "generate" the spirit, to reveal and communicate that "eschaton" without which the Church is but an institution among other human institutions... ."[105]

Liturgy certainly has its place; no one would expect Schmemann to deny that. But when liturgy generates this spirit of which he speaks, then liturgy is communicating the eschaton for our present experience, and that liturgical *locus* makes theology possible. So shall we conclude that eschatology is the object of theological concern? Schmemann is willing to say so: "It is possible to say that liturgical theology has as its proper domain or 'object' eschatology itself, which is revealed in its fullness through the liturgy."[106] However, this object of liturgical theology is not something beyond the world, or irrelevant to the world, or detached from the world, or in the world's future. And this eschatology that occupies theology's attention is not so much defined, as it is described, because it can be experienced now, dawning upon us in our deification and giving us an experience of the world's teleology, i.e., its design and purpose. Christian saints and teachers, according to Schmemann, defined the spiritual life simply as the acquisition of the Holy Spirit and testimony of the reality of the Kingdom of God.

> "[I]s it not strange that in the present discussions of renewal so little place is given to this testimony ...? Is it not the result again of a particular theological deformation, of another "disconnection": this time theology and spirituality? Is it not clear that the same theology which, in its triumphant intellectualism

ignored liturgy as the *locus theologicus par excellence*, had to ignore *ipso facto* spirituality? The latter was thus isolated in a particular compartment: that of "mysticism," and ruled out as a source of theology. What we discover today, however, is that theology, when reduced completely to a self-sufficient rational structure, becomes, in fact, defenseless in front of secular philosophies and finishes by accepting them as its own criterion and foundation. It literally cuts itself off from its sources, from that reality which alone makes "words about God" *theoprepeis*, i.e. adequate to God."[107]

Without liturgical piety, liturgical theology fails to be adequately done because liturgical mysticism is ruled out as a source of theology.

What Liturgical Piety Is

So let us turn to our second task, since we are already on the edge of it, and see what Schmemann *does* mean by liturgical piety. We can expect it will involve connecting liturgy and theology and spirituality. We can expect that liturgy will serve as the root and source of a piety that is nevertheless directed outward, toward the world, and not inward, toward itself. Schmemann says,

> "My point here is thus again a simple one. There can be no renewal in any area of Church life or, simply, of the Church herself, without first a spiritual renewal. But this emphatically is not a mere pietistic statement, a call for more prayer. It means, above everything else, the overcoming of the tragical divorce between the thought of the Church and the experience of the Kingdom of God, which is the only source, guide, and fulfillment of that thought, and the only ultimate motivation of all Christian action. At the risk of shocking many a Christian, one can say that the Church as *institution*, as *doctrine*, and as *action* has no ultimate meaning in itself. For all these point beyond

themselves to a reality which they represent and describe and seek, which is fulfilled, however, only in the new life, in the *koinonia* of the Holy Spirit."[108]

The reason that *lex orandi* is the foundation for theology and piety is the fact that liturgy is where we today experience the epiphany of the Kingdom. When Schmemann says the Church has no ultimate meaning in itself I think he means that in liturgy the eyes of the Church are not to be turned upon herself, immanently, but turned upward, eschatologically.

Liturgical piety is the *mysterion* showing up in our lives. Liturgical piety consists of the eschatological effects of the Kingdom, just celebrated in the liturgy, transfiguring the world to which we return after the celebration. We will discover piety's province when we remember that God so loved the world that he gave his Son for its life. Liturgical piety is this new life, which comes from Christ, which is facilitated by the Church, which arises in our conversion, which begins with our baptism into Christ, who empowers us with the Holy Spirit, who is the source of our spirituality. The Church's assigned mission, her *leitourgia,* is to witness to the transforming effects of the Kingdom of God by being transformed herself. To be a sacrament, the Church must be a sign, but she must be an efficacious sign. The Church shows the Kingdom of God not by pointing at some far off target at the end of history, but by displaying it *eschatologically.* Using the word as an adverb does not mean "later;" displaying the Kingdom *eschatologically* does not mean a finger pointing to an empty space that will be later occupied. *Eschatologically* means the Kingdom present, though still arriving; it means its dawning on earth. In her liturgy the Church displays the Kingdom *eschatologically.* When the transfiguring power of the liturgy makes a change in the theologian's life, then liturgical theology has been married to spirituality. Then we discover that the liturgy defines and judges our *pietas,* our duty and devotion toward God in our daily life. "The true significance of the Eucharist is precisely that of judgment, or transformation, of making infinitely important, the whole of life."[109] Because Christ has been introduced into time, all moments in time are filled with meaning and acquire their significance in relation to Christ.

Liturgical spirituality is not our accomplishment, it is the presence of the Holy Spirit within a baptized person. "Mystical" is not a character trait that only some people have. "Mystical" means that theology is made possible by the Church's experience of herself as communion of the Holy Spirit. The Church is communion of the Holy Spirit, and when the mystic is in communion with the Church, then his or her liturgical theology is by definition mystical. Therefore, our piety – our obedience or loyalty towards God – is driven outward, not inward, following the Holy Spirit on his evangelical mission. Liturgy is centrifugal, not centripetal. That is why Schmemann thinks the liturgical movement "has appeared everywhere closely bound up with a theological, missionary and spiritual revival. It has been the source of a greater realization by Christians of their responsibility in the world. It has been a revival of the Church herself."[110]

Liturgical reform should not, therefore, be self-serving; liturgical reform is a matter of empowering the Church's *leitourgia*, which is the work of a few on behalf of the many. We both celebrate God's eschatological action in the liturgical cult, and contemplate God's eschatological action in the world. Theology is a vision, but it is not a vision of the Church as institution or doctrine, it is vision of the Church as the spiritual reality of the *koinonia* that the Holy Spirit has been tasked to bring about. Liturgy should refer us to what Schmemann called the three inseparable realities of the Christian faith: *the world, the Church, and the Kingdom*, and these three are the concern of both liturgical theology and piety. They are inseparable because they are not so much three things, as they are one thing in process. The Church is the world in the course of transfiguration. Schmemann writes,

"The Church is not a natural community which is 'sanctified' through the cult. In its essence the Church is the presence, the actualization in this world of the 'world to come,' in this *aeon* – of the Kingdom."[111] She exists by the Kingdom's inroad into this life, i.e., she exists eschatologically. This actualization of new life is precisely the *leitourgia*, the duty, the mission laid upon the Church to convey to the world. Christians who are baptized into the service of the Church receive the duty (*pietas*) to be the presence of this new life in the world. Every baptized Christian is a martyr (witness); the font creates a reflex of evangelization.

Baptismal Foundations

Schmemann supposes that liturgical renewal involves the renewal of liturgical piety, and for that he suggests that we begin at the beginning: "with the restoration of Baptism as the liturgical act concerning the whole Church, as the very source of all liturgical piety which, in the past, was first of all a baptismal piety, a constant reference of the whole life to this mystery of its renewal and regeneration through the baptismal death and resurrection."[112] Liturgical piety refers our whole life to a share in Christ's three offices of prophet, priest, and king bestowed in baptism. Schmemann considers these three to be essential dimensions of genuine Christian spirituality, and when he comments on the last of them he is able to explain the cosmic dimension of our piety.

"Regenerating man, [the baptismal mystery] re-creates him as king, for to be king is his very nature. ... Thus if Christian life and spirituality have their source in baptismal regeneration, and if spirituality is above all the fulfillment by man of the gift received in Baptism, then the first and essential foundation and dimension of this actuality is established here, in this restoration of man as king. This means that it is primarily and essentially a *positive*, and not a negative, spirituality; that it stems from joy, acceptance and affirmation and not from fear, rejection and negation; that it is cosmic and doxological in its very content and orientation."[113] Spirituality consists of the edification, or building up, of the baptismal gifts that were given in order that we might cooperate in the renewal God intends for this world. That renewal is the Kingdom celebrated. That renewal celebrated is the Kingdom being present eschatologically. In the liturgy the accomplishment, establishment, growth, effect, inauguration, achievement, and realization of the Kingdom is celebrated, as the Holy Spirit extends the consequences of Christ's Paschal mystery to every corner of our lives, and every corner of the world. In other words, Christ saves us by restoring our nature, which inescapably makes us *part* of creation, and calls us to be its *kings*. He offers salvation *of* the world, not *from* the world, and he saves by making us again that which we are.[114]

This idea of being "made new" is crucial to Schmemann's thought, and it is crucial in our understanding if we are to grasp his concept of liturgical piety. The

Kingdom works upon the world by transfiguring something old into something new.

> "Christ never spoke of the natural and supernatural. He spoke rather of the old and the new, and especially the renovation of the old. Sacrament is movement, transition, passage, Pascha: Christ knows the way and guides us, going forth. The world, condemned in its old nature, revealed as life eternal in its new nature, is still the same world, God's good work. Christ came to save it, not to allow us means of thankful escape before it was discarded as rubbish."[115]

Christ came not to make a new world, but to make the world new; and our Christian spirituality does not ascend to gnostic heights and leave behind the material, historical, political world; Christian spirituality transforms it.

The purpose of the Christian community, that is, the Church's fullness, is growth in faith and love, knowledge and *koinonia.* This process of sanctification and growth in holiness is

> "the slow transformation of the old Adam in us into the new one, the restoration of the pristine beauty which was lost in sin, the illumination with the uncreated light of Mount Tabor. It is also the slow victory over the demonic powers of the cosmos, the "joy and peace" which *hinc et nunc* make us partakers of the Kingdom and of life eternal. The Orthodox spiritual tradition has always stressed the mystical nature of Christian life, as life "hidden with Christ in God.""[116]

Now that is a sight for sore eyes! That is a vision for the liturgical theologian, as he or she comprehends the world in a new way. The world is illuminated with the uncreated light of God radiating from liturgy, which is God extending his Kingdom eschatologically. This is liturgical piety in action.

But this is not easy for us because it threatens the Old Adam. The transformation of the Old Adam has a cost, and it is called mortification. The bridge by which we are to pass into this transfigured world is the cross, and we must lie down on it during our passage. It requires, as Schmemann said, a victory over the demonic powers, which is why I am inclined to talk about liturgical piety as "liturgical asceticism." In my opinion, most spirituality is presented as having all the consistency of a jellyfish; to the contrary, liturgical asceticism is vertebrate spirituality. This paper is about Schmemann's understanding, not mine, so I will not sidetrack us into what I think is the role of asceticism.[117] But I will pause to note that although some have said Schmemann had no place for asceticism in his "system,"[118] I found more references to asceticism in my preparation for this symposium than I thought I would find. Here are four. First, Schmemann names asceticism as a component of Byzantine Christianity. After naming the characteristics of truth and beauty, he says

"A third aspect of the Byzantine Christian culture can be adequately termed ascetical. Man's sin and alienation from God, the radical illness of "this world," the narrow way of salvation – these are the essential components of Byzantine religious experience. ... It is, as I said already, a "monastic" society in the sense that it accepts the monastic ideal as the self-evidence norm and criterion of all Christian life."[119]

Second, asceticism is a detachment required of each person. "There is every justification for that detachment, that abandonment of the world so heavily stressed in the ascetical tradition."[120] Third, it fundamental to the Church because "In this world the Church is 'possible' only as a 'station,' an expectation, a preparation, as an ascetical action."[121] And fourth, it is fundamental to Christian life. "There is no Christian life without *martyria* and without *asceticism*, this latter term meaning nothing else, fundamentally, but a life of concentrated effort and fight."[122] Other passages make it clear that Schmemann does not think spirituality comes without cost, and in my vocabulary, asceticism is the name for paying that price.

Since liturgical piety has an ascetical cost, we are much more comfortable talking about a reform of the liturgy than a reform of the liturgist. We are much more comfortable talking about a ritual reform than a personal reform. We are much more comfortable talking about a revival of *cult* than a revival of *culture*. Schmemann acknowledges this. He acknowledges that the Sunday morning churchgoers are not aware of the impact the liturgy is supposed to have upon their way of life.

"What they are not aware of is that the Byzantine liturgy – which they dutifully and in faithfulness to their Orthodox heritage attend on Sunday – by its every word and rite challenges the culture in which they live and which they enthusiastically adopt as their "way of life" Monday through Saturday; that the Orthodox faith which they so proudly confess on the Sunday of Orthodoxy contains and posits a vision of man, world, nature, matter, entirely different from the one which in fact shapes not only their lives but their mental and psychological makeup as well."[123]

Liturgical pietism is not an increased piety about the liturgy, not a call for more prayer, not an enthusiasm for cultus, it is rather letting the *mysterion* have an impact upon our world, namely, upon everything by which and in which we live. There is no boundary to our *pietas*, i.e., to the dutiful conduct we owe God. Our spirituality is the life of the Holy Spirit within us, and what range of interest does he have? The whole cosmos and the full span of history, every individual and every nation, our souls and our bodies, the Church and the world, material objects and spiritual verities. Liturgical theology provides us with a penetrating gaze into the ontological foundations of the world and its intended eschatological end, and any movement to renew liturgy is done in order to empower liturgical piety. Any liturgical renewal is done in order to sharpen our vision and fortify us to live by it.

Limiting the liturgical life of the Church to Sunday morning is a problem that Schmemann sees in his own Orthodox Church in America because liturgy exercises insufficient power over life.

"What I mean is the *power* of the liturgy, first, to impress on the soul of man the Orthodox vision of life and, second, to help him live in accordance with that vision. Or, to put it in simple terms, the influence of the liturgy on our ideas, decisions, behavior, evaluations – on the totality of our life. This was for centuries and centuries the real function of the liturgy in the Orthodox Church: to immerse the man in the spiritual reality, beauty and depth of the Kingdom of God and to *change* his mind and his heart. By revealing and manifesting the "bridal chamber adorned" the liturgy was revealing to man his exile and alienation from God and thus was bringing him to repentance, to the desire to return to God and do his commandments."[124]

For centuries and centuries the real function of the liturgy was to yield liturgical piety. Liturgical theology's purpose is to extend the power of the epiphany experienced in the liturgy to all our existence, and that is liturgy become spiritual.

Really, liturgical piety simply means the antithesis of secularism, the latter meaning life according to the world's values. Liturgical piety is the antithesis of worldliness, which I define as taking the world without reference to God. The mystery of iniquity is that we have somehow managed to make the world worldly. We do not need liturgy in our life in order to have a place where we can go to escape the world, we need liturgy in our life in order to receive the world again as it was given. Liturgy will change the world.

"The Church, the sacrament of Christ, is not a "religious" society of converts, an organization to satisfy the "religious" needs of man. It is new life and redeems therefore the whole life, the total being of man. And this whole life of man is precisely the world in which and by which he lives. Through man the Church saves and redeems the world. One can say that "this world" is saved and redeemed every time a man responds to the divine gift, accepts it and lives by it. ... The Kingdom is yet *to come*, and the Church is not *of* this world. And yet this kingdom to come is already present, and the Church is fulfilled *in* this world."[125]

By *liturgy* we are imbued with God's values, by *theology* we have a vision of God's intent, and by *spirituality* we imprint them upon every place in which and by which we live.

Cosmic Priesthood

Third, and finally, this understanding of liturgical piety is summed up in Schmemann's definition of man and woman as cosmic priest. Some people think that liturgy is the priest's special province; that is a correct instinct, but it is only rightly applied when we remember that man and woman were created priests in the world. There is, therefore, a liturgy after the liturgy,[126] a liturgy for the life of the world. A more expansive definition of liturgy results from an expanded definition of priesthood as an anthropological potentiality. Schmemann is excellent on this. Man and woman are to bless God for the food and life they receive, respond to God's blessing with their blessing, see the world as God sees it, name and possess the world.

> "All rational, spiritual and other qualities of man, distinguishing him from other creatures, have their focus and ultimate fulfillment in this capacity to bless

God, to know, so to speak, the meaning of the thirst and hunger that constitutes his life. *"Homo sapiens,"* *"homo faber"* ... Yes, but, first of all, *"homo adorans."* The first, the basic definition of man is that he is *the priest.*"[127]

The Fall of Adam and Eve was the forfeiture of their liturgical career. When life was no longer accepted at the hand of the Father, Adam and Eve tried to find life from the world of nature. Except the world of nature cannot provide it.

"The natural dependence of man upon the world was intended to be transformed constantly into communion with God in whom is all life. Man was to be the priest of a eucharist, offering the world to God. ... The world is meaningful only when it is the "sacrament" of God's presence. Things treated merely as things in themselves destroy themselves because only in God have they any life. The world of nature, cut off from the

source of life, is a dying world. For one who

thinks food in itself is the source of life, eating

is communion with the dying world, it is

communion with death. Food itself is dead, it

is life that has died and it must be kept in

refrigerators like a corpse."[128]

Liturgical spirituality is a resumption of that priesthood: going

about one's daily life in a liturgical manner. Liturgical

spirituality is living in the world as cosmic priest, a theme that

Schmemann uses to great effect.

"Man was created as a priest: the world was created as

the matter of a sacrament. But sin came, breaking this

unity: this was no mere issue of broken rules alone,

but rather the loss of a vision, the abandonment of a

sacrament. Fallen man saw the world as one thing,

secular and profane, and religion as something

entirely separate, private, remote and "spiritual." The

sacramental sense of the world was lost. Man forgot
the priesthood which was the purpose and meaning
of his life. He came to see himself as a dying organism
in a cold, alien universe."[129]

The vision lost was the theological vision of the world
as sacrament, but Christ's Paschal mystery restores that vision
to us. Sacramental liturgy enables mundane liturgy: the sacred
liturgy enables liturgy conducted in the profane. Priesthood
apparently exists in three forms: the ministerial priesthood,
the baptismal priesthood, and the cosmic priesthood. And the
purpose of the first is to edify the second so that Christians
can resume the third. Schmemann contrasts the two states,
original and fallen, as a choice between living as priest or
consumer.

"The first consumer was Adam himself. He chose not
to be priest but to approach the world as consumer:
to "eat" of it, to use and to dominate it for himself, to
benefit from it but not to offer, not to sacrifice, not

to have it for God and in God. And the most tragical fruit of that original sin is that it made religion itself into a "consumer good" meant to satisfy our "religious needs," to serve as a security blanket or therapy, to supply us with cheap self-righteousness and equally cheap self-centered and self-serving "spiritualities"..."[130]

When we abandoned our post as priest, the material world itself did not change (because Manichaeism is never correct), but the world did change *for us*.

"In the mythology of creation, man is created a hungry being; that is why God made the world as his food. Man is dependent; ... The priest is first and foremost the sacrificer .... And so he is the man who can freely transform that dependence: he is the man who can say *thank you*. For the moment when the slave whom God has created can thank Him for his life and for his food, he is liberated; sacrifice, the thank-offering is liberating. I've always understood the fall (or what is called "Original Sin") as the loss of man's desire to be a priest; or perhaps you might say the desire he has *not* to be a priest but a consumer...."[131]

Original Sin did not primarily manifest itself in the breaking of rules, it manifested itself in making everything topsy-turvy: religion became a consumer good, the spirit of Christ became a self-serving spiritualty, cult became retreat from life, faith became fantasy, sacrament became unnatural, our horizon shortened, the heavens were off bounds, the earth became resistant, time became an adversary, and original sin deprived the cosmos of its principal agents. The purpose of the piety that arises from liturgy is to untangle this mess.

In our transfigured state, the first restoration we undergo is a priesthood that restores the power of sacrifice. This is rehearsed in the Eucharist's complementary movements of ascending and returning, then those movements are put into practice in our mundane liturgy.

> "The Eucharist begins as an ascension toward the throne of God, toward the Kingdom. ... The Eucharist is offered "on behalf of all and for all," it is the fulfillment by the Church of its priestly function: the reconciliation of the whole creation with God, the sacrifice of the whole world to God, the intercession for the whole world before God. ... And then, precisely at the moment when this state of fullness has been reached and consummated at the table of the Lord in His Kingdom ... the second movement begins – that of *return into the world.* "[132]

The choreography we learn in the Eucharistic liturgy trains our feet in the path we walk in our daily *pietas*.

Conclusion

Let me conclude with a glance back over all three investigations: (i) should liturgy matter, (ii) where is theology done, and (iii) does liturgy enter our life? In these three questions we were only following Schmemann's own definition of the goal of liturgical theology, which is to overcome the fateful divorce between theology, liturgy, and piety. This breakup deprived liturgy of its proper understanding, theology of its living source, and piety of its living content. It would seem, then, that a binary connection is not enough for him (liturgy plus piety); even a *pair* of binary connections is not enough for him (liturgical theology plus liturgical piety); Schmemann wants a *trinary* connection (liturgy plus theology plus piety). He summarizes his point by saying, "To understand liturgy from inside, to discover and experience that 'epiphany' of God, world and life which the liturgy contains and communicates, to relate this vision and

this power to our own existence, to all our problems: such is
the purpose of liturgical theology."[133] In actual fact, there is a
kind of perichoresis between the three – liturgy, theology,
spirituality – but if we wanted to prioritize them in some
fashion, perhaps it is best to say that liturgy is the baseline of
the triangle. Liturgy is the place of the experience of the
Kingdom of God, making it the source for theology and
equally the source for a renewed spirituality. Failing this,
theology ceases to be of any concern to the lives of ordinary
Christians, as Schmemann is afraid has happened.

> "[Theology] has ceased to be *pastoral* in the sense of
> providing the Church with essential and saving
> norms; and it has also ceased to be *mystical* in the
> sense of communicating to the people of God the
> knowledge of God which is the very content of life
> eternal. A theology alienated from the Church, and
> the Church alienated from theology; such is the first
> dimension of today's crisis."[134]

I take it, then, that Mrs. Murphy the liturgist turns out to be not only a theologian, but also a mystic. The liturgical theology that persons such as herself do is "'description' more than 'definition' for it is, above all, a search for words and concepts adequate to and expressive of the living experience of the Church; for a reality and not 'propositions.'"[135]

The liturgical cult does not exist for itself, it exists for the sake of the world, for the sake of understanding and transforming the world. This antinomous presence of the eschaton turns the liturgy inside out so it can spill into life as piety. This gives the Christian cult a different function than the function of any other cult on the face of the planet, at any time in history.

"[The specificity of the Christian *leitourgia*] consists in the *eschatological* character of the Christian cult whose essential "function" is to *realize* the church by revealing her as the epiphany of the Kingdom of

God. In this sense the Christian cult is unique, without analogies and without antecedents within the universal phenomenon of religious cult. ... For this "uniqueness" of the Christian cult comes to it exclusively from the Christian faith which, if it is on the one hand a belief comparable to all other beliefs, is on the other hand the possession and the experience of the object of this belief: the Kingdom of God itself. ... And it is the liturgy which accomplishes this presence in this *parousia* ..."[136]

Because in liturgy Mrs. Murphy experiences the Kingdom eschatologically, she experiences the world differently. "One can say that the uniqueness, the radical novelty of the new Christian leitourgia was here, here, in this 'entrance' into the Kingdom which for 'this world' is still 'to come,' but of which the Church is truly the sacrament: the beginning, the anticipation, and the 'parousia.'"[137]

Part II

In the three chapters above we let Schmemann explain his understanding of liturgy, theology, and piety – the three components that he says liturgical theology must reunite. We tried to show how liturgy matters outside the Church, how theology can be done outside the academy, and why we need liturgy in our life.

Upon this foundation laid by Schmemann we could now turn our eyes to two applications of liturgy: first concerning the consecration of the world, and second the interplay of liturgy, theology and asceticism. The two concluding chapters come from my voice, but not without echoes of Schmemann.

Chapter 4: Liturgy and the Consecration of the World

As I've gotten older, I increasingly believe that we think in metaphors and images much more than we think in propositions, and even though I'm going to use up an hour of oxygen making some propositions, I believe it is the image itself that you will remember instead of anything I say. I will enter it through a question: What is the difference between a circle and a wheel? There is really nothing different about their shape; a wheel *is* circular. Yet the distinguishing feature of a wheel is that it is a circle that touches the ground. A wheel moves forward as it turns, while a circle could be turning, suspended in the air. A circle spins, but a wheel turns; a circle revolves, but a wheel advances; a circle remains where it is even while it orbits, but because the wheel is pressed against the earth it makes progress when it turns. The two are similar in many ways, yet they are drastically different in this particular way.

Now, by means of my image I propose that although many people see liturgy as a circle, liturgy is better understood as a wheel. I'm going to try to bring us from a circular understanding of liturgy to a wheeled understanding.

Let me return to my picture of the circle. Imagine it hanging there in the air. It could be spinning fast or slow, but this doesn't matter because its revolution does not affect anything nearby. If the circle were a cog, its teeth would not be engaging any other gears to turn them in the machine. It is elegant, as all circles are; it has a geometric beauty that comes from the mathematical logic of points exactly equidistant from the center point. We can imagine Plato taking out his compass and drawing one circle after another, just because its ideality pleases him. The fact that it is round gives it a kind of eternal perfection – a perfect beauty – and although circles come in many sizes, the circle is a universal shape.

Some people seem to picture liturgy as a circle. They see the liturgy turning, but they don't see it going anywhere.

They are impressed by its perfect beauty, even if it does not perform any labor. We can imagine an ecclesiastical Plato taking out his rubrical compass and tracing one liturgy after another, just because its perfect liturgical form is pleasing to him. But what difference does the circular liturgy make? Only certain kinds of people take interest in the liturgical sphere. People with a refined aesthetic taste might find it a relaxing home in which to investigate art and music; the canon lawyer would like to know how to maintain that perfect shape, and rubricists would help him with matters of orderliness; historians might possibly be drawn into the liturgical loop to see how it was expressed in various cultures. But all of these seem fairly rarefied interests. More hardheaded, down to earth, practical and pragmatic people would take less interest in the spinning circle. Why would a dogmatician care about liturgy if he thought it was only the expression of a theology of a particular group? Why would a moralist care about liturgy when it occurs in the heavens above, and not at the center of the polis? Why would most of the secular world care about the liturgical twirl that Christians take in the temple once a week (like whirling dervishes) when those Christians seem to return to the world looking the same way they did when they left it?

Even people who are on the side of liturgy, and want to defend its value, understand that there is a risk that liturgy will be perceived this way, and somewhere in their writing they take the time to protest it. Pius XII writes in his encyclical *Mediator Dei* that it is an error and a mistake "to think of the sacred liturgy as merely the outward or visible part of divine worship or as an ornamental ceremonial. No less erroneous is the notion that it consists solely in a list of laws and prescriptions according to which the ecclesiastical hierarchy orders the sacred rites to be performed."[138] In his famous 1964 open letter to the Liturgical Conference Romano Guardini admits that "the efforts of those who concerned themselves with the liturgy must have appeared as peculiarities of aesthetes who lacked Christian sincerity."[139] And Lambert Beauduin was disheartened by the fact that although he was invited to speak at a conference, he "experienced difficulty in finding a section under which to hold his speech. He was rejected three times by the sections on doctrine, morality, and piety. He finally came to be listed under 'art' with the subsection 'liturgy and religious music.'"[140] Liturgy was not taken seriously, it was just a matter of aesthetics. Even I have registered my complaints about the mentality of the circle when I wrote about the time I was waiting in line for commencement exercises, dressed in academic cap and gown, and a colleague who knew my interest in liturgy said to me, "You must like this sort of thing." He had concluded that since I was interested in liturgy I would enjoy excessive pomp, useless formality, ritual etiquette, and extravagant ceremony.[141] Such a liturgy spins above our heads, making no particular contact with our world.

I hope to propose a different view of liturgy for you today, picturing it for the remainder of our time as a wheel. It is still circular, possessing that perfection of eternity, but with this difference: it moves when it rotates because it is touching the ground of our lives. If the liturgy is not to be just an endless circle of public ceremonial, but is to have some consequence, then I must put the question to each of us: where on earth does liturgy land? Where in our lives can this liturgical circle touch down, and toward what end does the liturgy move? Paul spoke about a "weight of glory" (2 Cor 4:17) bearing down upon us and stirring our souls; I want to suggest that there is a "weight of liturgy" that grounds our lives.

I suggest four groundings, four places where the circle becomes a wheel, four points of gravity where the weight of liturgy brings it into contact with our life. Liturgy presses upon *matter* in such a way that the cosmos becomes sacramental; it presses upon *anthropology* in such a way as to reveal our cosmic priesthood; it presses upon our *hearts* in such a way that our liturgical spirituality becomes a sequel of Christ; and it presses upon *history* in such a way that the axle of this wheel can carry eschatological freight.

1. Liturgy and cosmos

There are not two liturgies, one in heaven and one on earth; there is one liturgy, in heaven and on earth. But far from making liturgy into an escape hatch for evacuating the world, I mean the exact opposite: liturgy is Jacob's ladder revisited, with two-directional traffic ascending and descending. It is a ladder that Christ's incarnation constructed. Liturgy gives matter its telos, like an acorn finds its telos in the oak, a child finds his telos in adulthood. You know that the word "matter" is connected to *mater*: to ask, "what does it matter?" is to ask "to what does it give birth?" Philosophers have always suspected that this world is but a shadow of a deeper, thicker, higher reality, but it required Christianity to remind the philosophers that the dawning of that reality is not at the expense of the material world. Heaven is based on the resurrection of the body, not escaping from it. This world matters: eternal things are gestated there and given birth. Alexander Schmemann insisted on this:

"Christ never spoke of the natural and supernatural. He spoke rather of the old and the new, and especially the renovation of the old. Sacrament is movement, transition, passage, Pascha: Christ knows the way and guides us, going forth. The world, condemned in its old nature, revealed as life eternal in its new nature, is still the same world, God's good work. Christ came to save it, not to allow us means of thankful escape before it was discarded as rubbish."[142]

Space, time, and matter are a three-sided loom on which real life is woven, one day to be gently lifted off by the master weaver, without dropping a stitch, to be fitted into his own radiant garment.[143]

And that is what is celebrated in liturgy when earth and heaven kiss. Liturgy is the point where two arcs touch, and glory meets doxology. It is the gate through which the glory of heaven floods the earth, and by which the worship of the cosmos ascends to glorify God. First the downward motion: the Fathers said that when the heavenly angels saw their Prince "tarrying among the places of earth, they entered by the way that He had opened, following their Lord. ... They said among themselves, 'If He has put on mortal flesh, how can we remain doing nothing? Come, angels, let us all descend from heaven.'"[144] That's why the Christmas sky was filled with angels. Second the ascending motion: Irenaeus writes, "Seeing him approach, the lower angels cried out to those who were above them, 'Open your gates; rise up, ye gates of eternity; the King of Glory will enter.' And when the angels from above asked in their astonishment, 'Who is He?' those who saw Him cried out anew, 'It is the Lord, strong and mighty. It is the King of Glory.'"[145] The angels doubted when they saw Christ arise in the flesh because his body did not have these marks of suffering when he first descended, so Gregory Nazianzen advises that we "Show them the beautiful tunic of the Body which suffered, and how it has grown even more beautiful in His Passion and has been made to reflect the shining glory of the Godhead."[146] The risen and ascended Christ keeps his embodied humanity, and performs liturgy with it at the right hand of the Father.

Heaven bows down and kisses earth, earth stretches upwards and embraces heaven. Why, it's almost like they were made for each other. The result is delight at an ontological level. This is happiness that occurs at the level of being, that is, from the fulfillment of a hunger for union built into the nature of things. In the liturgy we experience the union intended between the spiritual and the corporeal, the invisible and the visible, the mystical and the mundane, the divine and the human, the uncreated and the created. In order to arrive at this joy, liturgical union bases itself upon the hypostatic union in Christ. In his person (hypostasis) was the union of divine nature and human nature without confusion, separation, change, or division. He united the Uncreated and the created, and what he did in his historical person is perpetuated in and through his mystical body. Just as Christology taught us to neither emphasize his humanity at the expense of his divinity, nor his divinity at the expense of his humanity, so we are taught by the liturgy to not overemphasize either dimension of the Church. The Church is neither just a human Jesus Club, socially organized to meet my needs, nor something hidden, invisible, and merely future. The liturgy is designed both to lift me up into transcending realities, and to transfigure space, time, and matter. This is because the liturgy follows the trail of the hypostatic union, wherein nature is perfected by grace, spirit rules flesh, humanity is sanctified, the cosmos becomes sacramental, sacred matter becomes a foretaste of the heavenly banquet, and profane matter is constructed into an image of the kingdom of God in our very midst.

Sacred and profane need not be opposed. The sacred is a schoolhouse in which we learn our lessons, but it is not time wasted. We do not practice arithmetic in the schoolhouse so that it can stay there; we practice it so the skill can come out with us for daily use. Likewise, when we practice the sacred geometry taught us in the temple, it is not so it remains there; we practice the skill so it can become our life's design. Sometimes a biased reading of the Old Testament opposes sacred and profane in the persons of priest and prophet, but I think the prophet does not mind someone going into the temple – the prophet is only bothered if a person does not take the temple *with him* when he comes back out. He is critical if what has been tilled in the sacred cult does not cultivate a seed taking root in the daily world.

When spirit meets matter, the former imprints the latter. Matter is not left behind as the scale of being is ascended. For example, the cells of our bodies are organized in such a way as to serve our soul, our rational life. For example, at one level a meal simply serves a biological need for nutrition, but at a higher level a meal can be a family fellowship or a romantic banquet (and at the highest level, a meal of bread and wine can be the sacramental veil of real communion with God Almighty). All the sacraments use matter to touch the soul. Water regenerates new being, a vow bonds permanently, bread and wine feed immortality, a confessor perfects penitence, oil recuperates the soul, hand laying consecrates to service, and oil inspires (I don't mean it gets us worked up, I mean that the Spirit is breathed into us).

But my point is not simply to speak of the sacraments *within* the liturgy, I am also thinking of how the *liturgy after the liturgy* finds the world to have been made different. Wittgenstein said – I paraphrase – that the world of the happy person must look completely different from the world of the unhappy person. I propose that the world of the liturgist looks completely different from the world of the sinner. The world becomes sacramental and sacrificial when the weight of liturgy touches down in it. In every century, Christian theology has had to combat a form of Manichaeism, and insist that the problem is not matter but our treatment of it. No thing is sinful, but any thing can be used sinfully. If liturgy is to touch our lives, it must rub against our bodies as well as our souls. St John Paul II writes, "Christianity does not reject matter. Rather, bodiliness is considered in all its value in the liturgical act, whereby the human body is disclosed in its inner nature as a temple of the Spirit and is united with the Lord Jesus, who himself took a body for the world's salvation."[147] Christ's incarnation in body, and the resurrection of his body, and the ascension of that glorified body means that this present age is a chrysalis for hatching a new age when God's glory will saturate our bodies. Bodies possess unique dignity, which is why Christians are moved to protect them from conception to natural death.

The liturgical purpose of matter is twofold. First, all material things can become *sacramental* because they can serve as a theophany of God's grace; and second, all material things can become *sacrificial* because they can be used in our response to that grace. We live in a forest of sacramental and sacrificial realities. The rule of Benedict says "let him regard all utensils of the monastery and its whole property as if they were the sacred vessels of the altar."[148] When someone understands that all the tools he has been given for work, for play, for service, for self-help have come from the hand of God, then he treats his tools for living with the fond attentiveness given to something sacred. This is the inhaling and exhaling of liturgy, the sacramental and sacrificial sides of liturgy, the traditional twin purposes of sanctifying persons and glorifying God. The light of Mount Tabor streams from every liturgy's home base, the altar, then permeates the citizens of the nave, and then flows through the narthex in order to reveal the material world's primordial potential. Then we see both matter and our neighbor the way God sees them, in a light that comes from God. The Catechism of the Catholic Church puts it thus:

> "Purity of heart is the precondition of the vision of God. Even now it enables us to see *according to* God, to accept others as "neighbors"; it lets us perceive the human body – ours and our neighbor's – as a temple of the Holy Spirit, a manifestation of divine beauty (CCC, no. 2519)".

When the Christian liturgist returns across that same narthex boundary a week later, it is to bring his whole world back to the altar in thankful oblation. Every Sunday, every eighth day, the liturgists drag behind themselves the goods and virtues they have collected over the past week: their marriage, the civitas they have been building, the culture they have been constructing, the beauties they have enjoyed, the sorrows they have endured, and they deliver their world to the foot of the altar. There is bidirectional traffic in every liturgy. Within the sacred sphere we glimpse under sacramental veil the homage that matter can pay to God – water, oil, bread, hand laying, icon, incense, brick and glass, assembled bodies. Having seen this, we treat all material objects with new reverence. But this already leads me to my second point. Everything that I've been saying about the potential of matter depends upon man and woman recovering their liturgical identity.

2. Liturgy and Anthropology

Why do we fail to see the universe as cosmic sacrament? It is not the fault of God; it is not the fault of matter; the fault is in the eye of the beholder. Our eyes have grown dim by the cataract of sin we inherited from our Original Parents, darkening our view of the material world so that we no longer see it as the theophany that God intends every creature to be. The material world that should be an icon, a window, a door to the Creator instead becomes a distraction, then a temptation, then an object of idolatry. Our sight is impeded, and we no longer see through the creature to the Creator. So in order to see the world *outside* the temple as sacrament, our eyes must be healed by the sacraments administered *inside* the temple. The disease is spiritual, but it affects our treatment of matter. Likewise, the cure is spiritual, and it affects our treatment of matter.

Christ is the way, the truth, and the life: he is the king, the prophet, and the priest. And these offices he shares with all of his baptized liturgists, recovering a lost liturgical anthropology. Our self-understanding, our identity, our human responsibility can feel the weight of liturgy pressing upon it when liturgy challenges our personhood. To be a *prophet* means to see a particular circumstance in the light of God's law; to be a *priest* means to serve as a mediator; and to be a *king* means to rule as God's steward. Man and woman's liturgical identity is exercised in their vocation to discern the plan of God and execute it as royal priests. We have difficulty doing this now because the fall was the forfeiture of our liturgical career. If our liturgical humanity is to be restored, then the liturgy must penetrate us to the core, and reconstruct our identity as cosmic priests. In class, Aidan Kavanagh would define liturgy as "doing the world the way the world was meant to be done," and man and woman are transfiguring agents because of their anthropological identity as liturgist.

It is an amazing feature in the Judeo-Christian doctrine of creation that God freely shares this power and responsibility with the highest of his created beings. He does not begrudge it, and they do not have to steal it, as Prometheus stole fire from Zeus. God has gladly given dominion to man and woman, and it comes to them in the form of stewardship. They are royal priests. The fact that they are *priest* means they serve a ministry to God standing under obedience and serving a will other than their own. The fact that they are *royal* means that they serve a ministry to their fellow creatures over whom they have been made stewards, overseers, and managers. Lose the priestly identity, and in their hubris they will make their own plans for how the world can serve them; lose the royal identity, and they will leave vacant the governing keystone that upholds the created universe. Humanity must neither corrupt the order of things, nor abdicate their office.

The Old Testament prophets were constantly reminding the earthly king that he was only a steward, and as steward he was not the high king himself, he was looking after resources of the true High King. When Aslan crowns Caspian in the Chronicles of Narnia, he says "Under us and under the High King, you shall be King of Narnia, Lord of Cair Paravel, and Emperor of the Lone Islands."[149] Why this was done has already been explained by the badger Trufflehunter: "We beasts remember, even if Dwarfs forget, that Narnia was never right except when a son of Adam was

King. … It's not Men's country, but it's a country for a man to be King of. We badgers have long enough memories to know that."[150] In old English (which Lewis knew from his day job teaching medieval literature), *caer* meant court, and *paravail* meant lesser, or under. King Peter and Queen Lucy ruled at Cair Paravel over Narnia, but they ruled under Aslan, as we must also do. If we do not acknowledge a King above us, then we are tempted to slip onto the throne for ourselves, and then we will have every bit as much reason to be concerned about our job performance as did the man in Luke 16. "A rich man had a steward who was reported to him for squandering his property. He summoned him and said, 'What is this I hear about you? Prepare a full account of your stewardship …'" One day we will be summoned by the High King and asked to prepare a full account of our stewardship; he will ask us whether we have done the world righteously, prudently, justly. If a person thought he would never answer to the High King, I suppose that person would live differently; he would eat, he would drink, he would be merry, for tomorrow it ends. But if someone believed this eschatological judgment will come, he might step into the King's sacred home from time to time to pay homage and remember the shape of the true hierarchy. The liturgy presses down upon our anthropology, our identity as *anthropos*, and keeps it from becoming misshapen.

The liturgy stretches each man and woman taut between Genesis and Revelation so they can remember their original command and can be led to their daily response. More than being simply led to this response, they are sacramentally equipped for it. The sacramental strength received in liturgy enables us to do the world rightly, instead of sinfully. Our bent spines and stiff necks are realigned every eighth day. This weekly liturgical chiropracty straightens our posture so we can walk with the human dignity we were meant to have as we rule earth and air and beast and bird. That's why our governing needs a liturgical counter-weight.

Chesterton said it well when he described sacrifice among the Greeks:

> "[Greek sacrifice] did satisfy a thing very deep in humanity indeed; the idea of surrendering something as the portion of the unknown powers; of pouring out wine on the ground, of throwing a ring into the sea; in a word, of sacrifice. It is the wise and worthy idea of not taking our advantage to the full; of putting something in the other balance to ballast our dubious pride, of paying tithes to nature for our land. ...Where that gesture of surrender is most magnificent, as among the great Greeks, there is really much more idea that the man will be the better for losing the ox than that the god will be the better for getting it."[151]

Liturgy forms the humility proper to royalty. Everyone knows from fairy tales that arrogant kings and queens are going to get their comeuppance.

3. Liturgy and Hearts

The weight of the liturgy also presses upon our spirits, creating a liturgical spirituality. Men and women have a natural desire for the spiritual, but sin has affected every part of us, including our desires, and so liturgy must press upon us in order to give spiritual regulation to our hearts. I don't mean regulation in the sense of rules, I mean a regulated rhythm that smooths out rapid and irregular heartbeats. Liturgy is the heart of the world beating without sin's arrhythmia. This arrhythmia, of course, is what the ascetical tradition meant by the passions. The passions do not come with our nature, they are instances of where our natural faculties misfire. According to the arrangement made by Evagrius of Pontus we have three faculties, and each of them can miscarry. When the appetitive faculty is misdirected it yields the passions of gluttony, lust, and avarice; when the irascible or spirited faculty is misdirected it yields the passions of anger, despondency, and sloth; and when the intellective faculty is misdirected it yields the passions of vainglory and pride. Maximus the Confessor defines a passion as a movement of the soul contrary to nature, and so concludes that sin, in every case, is a misuse. It manifests in three ways: we misuse the world, we misuse our neighbor, and, incredible as it seems, we even misuse God himself.

First, we *misuse the world* by the appetitive passions. As I keep reminding my students, there is nothing wrong with money, sex, or beer – the problem is avarice, lust, and gluttony. As already mentioned, all things in the world are good, but in the hands of egocentric people all things in the world risk being used in the wrong way, for the wrong reason, in the wrong measure, at the wrong time. Second, these passions tempt us to *misuse our neighbor*: anger makes us draw back from communion, envy stirs us to sullen gossip, despondency saps our courage to address ills. Maximus says, "It happens that the passions of the irascible part of the soul are harder to combat than those of the concupiscible. Thus it is that a better remedy for it was given by the Lord: the commandment of love."[152] And third, incredibly, the intellective passions lead us to *misuse God* by supplanting him and dismissing him from our court. Selfish pride has an element of idolatry to it. Evagrius describes the demon of pride as inducing "the monk to deny that God is his helper and to consider that he himself is the cause of virtuous actions."[153] Vainglory is only the desire to boast of our achievements, but when that achievement is salvation, then we are talking about pride. The Lord of the Universe is unimpressed.

Liturgical asceticism repairs and realigns these faculties, restoring our capacity for worship. Liturgical asceticism perfects our natural spirituality, taking us out of our egocentrism. No longer sourced in our own religiousness, our spirituality comes to be sourced in Christ. The Spirit breathes in us: we con-spire with the Holy Spirit. Liturgical spirituality is a con-spiracy. This cannot be accomplished by our own religious efforts, which is why the spirituality of the least in the kingdom of God is greater than the spirituality of the greatest born of woman. The imitation of Christ occurs by a different power than my imitation of Socrates, or Marcus Aurelius, or St. Augustine. Since the prototype is the Son of God, therefore my spirituality must be more than moral mimicry or philosophical assent. Because Christ is something more, my imitation must be something different.

The tradition has called this "sequela Christi": each liturgist is baptized in order to become a sequel of Christ. Joseph Ratzinger describes it this way.

"The Sequela of Christ has a much higher goal: to be assimilated into Christ, that is to attain union with God. ... Man is not satisfied with solutions beneath the level of divinization. But all the roads offered by the "serpent" (Genesis 3:5), that is to say, by mundane knowledge, failed. The only path is communion with Christ, achieved in the sacramental life. The Sequela of Christ is not a question of morality, but a "mysteric" theme – an ensemble of divine action and our response."[154]

The path liturgical spirituality follows is communion with Christ. When liturgy integrates our asceticism, then something more than morality results: now we are talking about deification. Nature is perfected by grace, therefore our natural spirituality is perfected by being elevated to deification. It is more than we could have hoped for – but is that not always the way with grace? The risen, liturgical Christ assimilates us into himself in order that we may share his union with the Father through the Spirit. Liturgical spirituality is the Spirit living in us, bestowed by the power of the sacramental life that puts us on a path toward union with the Trinity. Now we have discovered the purpose – the end – not only of our individual lives but the purpose of creation itself. The Greek word *oikonomia* meant a "household management," and we have learned toward what end God has been managing his cosmos.

4. Liturgy and History

This brings us to the fourth point, one at which the circle touches down to wheel through history itself. The liturgical activity of God invades history in order to sweep us up and take us home to him. Liturgical transportation is like Elijah's chariot of fire, except it is a roomy vehicle, reminiscent of Noah's ark, that does not pluck us out alone, but brings along the identity that we have accumulated over the course of our lives.

Does time have a purpose? Are we really going nowhere but round and round? The medieval thinkers spoke of a goddess Fortuna who acted randomly, arbitrarily, aimlessly. They assigned her a "wheel of fortune," but by the grammar I'm using in this paper, I'm sure you will understand why I would rather call it a "*circle* of fortune." She changes the positions of people on this circle at random, and distributes failure and success without any rhyme or reason. Where is she going? She does not know because she is blind. And all we can be certain of is a final turn, when death will come unexpectedly. The threat of chronic meaninglessness (I mean the meaninglessness of *chronos*) can only be conquered if death itself is overcome, and that can only be done by someone who joins us in time, is our historical companion, enters Hades at his end, too, but bursts out from the inside, unhinging death's gates. That's exactly what the icons of resurrection show. That's exactly what the liturgy ceaselessly intones: the Greek Paschal troparion sings, "Christ is risen from the dead, trampling down death by death, and to those in the tomb bestowing life;" the second Latin Eucharistic Prayer sings, "he stretched out his hands as he endured his Passion, so as to break the bonds of death and manifest the resurrection;" and the Lutheran Church sings, "believing the witness of his resurrection, we await his coming in power to share with us the great and promised feast." Now we are getting somewhere! Now each moment, each day, each year inches forward to its telos. The ups and downs, the setbacks and delays, the troughs and peaks, the temporal and temporary character of our existence, do not trip us up: we are moving forward toward eternity, toward beatitude. Christ has aimed history toward its intended target.

We have all had the experience of throwing a stick out into the ocean and watching the waves push it back to shore eventually. To an impatient observer it can look as though the stick is barely moving forward at all, and is instead only rising and falling on repetitive, cyclical waves. But in actual fact, the wave's energy does move a small amount of water forward in each cycle, eventually bringing the stick back to land. There are recurring cycles in our life, but underneath them is an eschatological current. Feel for it. The philosophers spoke of a going out and coming back, called an *exitus* and a *reditus*, but they despaired over the wasted trip. For them, *exitus* was a disastrous fall from spiritual existence into material existence. Therefore, when Christians took up the idea they had to first of all clarify that the *exitus* was something thoroughly positive: it was the Creator's willed establishment of non-divine being. The Gospel's effect upon cosmology is to understand the cosmic circle to be wheeling toward its Creator. Ratzinger summarizes,

> "The *exitus*, or rather God's free act of creation, is indeed ordered toward the *reditus*, but that does not now mean the rescinding of created being. ... The creature, existing in its own right, comes home to itself, and this act is an answer in freedom to God's love. It accepts creation from God as his offer of love, and thus ensues a dialogue of love, that wholly new kind of unity that love alone can create. ... This *reditus* is a 'return', but it does not abolish creation; rather, it bestows its full and final perfection."[155]

The stick comes back to shore bigger; the spiral galaxy is released into space to take its turns, subject to the will of its

Creator, in order to accumulate being and return with a history. There is only one creature who fails this law of nature, and that is the spiritual creature who is capable of rebellion. For that creature, "the arch from *exitus* to *reditus* is broken. The return is no longer desired..."[156] Therefore, worship must now include a new aspect. Before we can make our worship, we must find purification, atonement, and deliverance from estrangement. Our wounded freedom must be healed. Then, at last, our sacrifice can be restored and perfected because our desire to offer the oblation to God will have been restored and perfected.

When this conversion happens, time changes – and I mean both cosmic time and every hour of our day. There is a goal, and that goal is to become a saint. A person is a verb (human *being*) until he or she becomes a noun (saint). By the light that bursts out the doors of the temple to flood the world in transfiguring light, the liturgist sees the cosmos theologically, as gift from God; he sees man and woman finally, fully, in their role as cosmic priests; time has now become a training school for eternal happiness; time now moves with a purpose, namely, to bring us a little closer to the Mystery which God has prepared for us, and for which he has been preparing us. Each passing day, each passing year, is not a tiresome cycle. Instead, liturgical time can carry us forward on the wheels of history to judgment. Paul Claudel says that we desire it, because our lives are in disarray without this terminus.

> "How long is it that we have just been jogging along, just jogging along? How long have we been piling up inside us, stuffing inside us like soiled linen in a suitcase, one on top of the other … things, people, memories, wishes, impressions, books, talks, opinions, successes, failures, humiliations, vices, good deeds, bad deeds."[157]

He adds that even in our memories these are not dead things, but alive and kicking and wriggling, and "we know all too well what happens on sleepless nights, for instance, when the whole lot starts stirring and pushing and screaming at once." This brings Claudel to a remarkable conclusion:

> "Our conscience has found what it longed for above all else: a Judge … There are so many things heaped up inside us already and only waiting to become an answer for the question to be put. A question, challenge, a presence. …
>
> Only profound emotion, the weight and painful pressure of harsh and turbulent events, reach down to the gushing salutary vein in the depths of us. Someone has fought his way through to us. Someone is urging us to say outright the real name, our own real name."[158]

We are answers in progress, waiting for the true question to be put to us. Who has it? Who can ask the question of us that unlocks the purpose of our accumulated life? What will it sound like? We catch an inkling at each liturgy where we have a foretaste of this eschatological judgment. The return has begun.

Conclusion

The Orthodox temple topography sees the sanctuary as heaven, the nave as the Church, and the narthex as the liminal boundary with the world. I have increasingly come to see the narthex as a membrane, and a permeable one at that. It is a barrier to the entry of certain things, like sin, death, despair, lovelessness, hatred, and so forth. As we cross the narthex going in, these should be sieved out of us with screens of finer and finer mesh. That is the spiritual life in action. But as we cross the narthex going back out, we bring with us new sight so we can see with the eye of the Dove, new hearts so we can order our affections, new respiration so we can breathe with the Spirit, new minds patterned after Christ who did not count equality with God a thing to be grasped, new hands that are open in *orans* and not clenched tight round some bauble, we become the sweet aroma of

Christ among those who are being saved and those who are perishing (2 Cor 2:15). In other words, we are made a new person. And that seems a worthwhile reason to step into the liturgical dance conducted for our benefit every week.

Chapter 5: On Liturgy, Theology and Asceticism

Ordinarily, it should not be necessary to tie a lecture as closely to the speaker as I'm going to do here. That is, ordinarily a speaker should be able to deliver a lecture without the audience having to know how he came to the topic, his personal commitments to the topic, or the value he places on the topic. But when the topic is liturgical theology, and I am the speaker, then these conditions impose themselves. This gracious invitation from the University of Lund leads me to reflect on my understanding of the nature, merit, and consequence of liturgical theology, and that is most easily explored by hanging it upon a biographical hook. It has been three and a half decades since I submitted a dissertation to my board with the terse and descriptive title of "What Is Liturgical Theology?" That was the question I confronted then, and I have continued to answer it for myself during the intervening years. As an outline for this paper, then, let me propose the metaphor that my graduate studies laid the foundation for a house which I have been building ever since. There is no pressure for you to live here, but I enjoy the opportunity to give you a tour of where I daily dwell.

The concrete of this foundation was poured by two persons, and you might guess their names. Fr. Alexander Schmemann was an Orthodox priest and Russian émigré, the product of St Sergius Orthodox Theological Institute in Paris, then scholar and dean of St. Vladimir's Orthodox Seminary in Crestwood, New York, from 1951 until his death in 1983. This was the time I was just beginning my graduate school education, and I did not yet know how important he would be to me, and I never met him. He outlined his thinking in a 1962 dissertation titled *Introduction to Liturgical Theology*, but his natural curiosity and concern for seminary education enlarged his scope of topics. Fr. Aidan Kavanagh was a convert to Catholicism, a Benedictine monk of St Meinrad's Archabbey in southern Indiana, though he spent most of his career elsewhere. After a dissertation in Trier and briefly teaching at

St Meinrad's he came to Notre Dame to direct the graduate liturgical studies program, but left for Yale University in 1974 where he taught until his retirement. One eager student appeared at his door in 1982 – myself – who pestered him for a directed readings course. He agreed on the condition that we read everything we could by Schmemann. We must respect the differences between these two men, but they are joined together in my experience and in contributing to what many have called a revolution in liturgical studies. In what way a revolution?

Up to this point, liturgy was generally found in one of three locations in the academy. Either it was a pastoral subject for clergy who were being taught how to preside at liturgy, and it was essentially a study in rubrics; or it was a subject for the comparative study of ritual, and it was essentially a study in history; or it was a topic for professors to write about as they proposed their view of a theology of worship, and it was basically illustrative. Schmemann took a totally new starting point when he asserted that theology takes place in the liturgy, and that liturgy is the basis for theology to occur. He wrote,

> "The formula *lex orandi est lex credendi* means nothing else than that theology is *possible* only within the Church. ... The problem of the relationship between liturgy and theology is not for the Fathers a problem of priority or authority. Liturgical tradition is not an 'authority' or a *locus theologicus;* it is the ontological condition of theology, of the proper understanding of *kerygma,* of the Word of God."[159]

I had to ask what he meant.

Kavanagh capitalized on the idea by claiming that the adjustment the community undergoes in liturgy "is theology being born, theology in the first instance. It is what tradition has called *theologia prima.*"[160] For him this meant taking seriously the verb in the original saying, often omitted in casual quotation, when someone refers to "*lex orandi, lex credendi.*" There the two phrases are only connected by a comma. But Prosper of Acquitaine's phrase contains a relational reference – *lex supplicandi legem statuat credendi* – from which Kavanagh concludes,

> "the predicate *statuat* does not permit these two fundamental laws to float apart or be opposed to each other. The verb *statuat* articulates the standard of believing and standard of worshiping within the faithful assembly. ... To reverse the maxim, subordinating the standard of worship to the standard of belief, makes a shambles of the dialectic of revelation."[161]

I had to ask what he meant, too.

So the basement to my house was laid when liturgy was given a more fundamental role in theology. Indeed, liturgy was given a foundational role. I had come as a systematic theologian who had indulged himself with one master's degree in liturgical history, and what I was planning to do was dissect the liturgy – kill it, pin it open on a board, and see the makeup of its internal organs – in order to understand some systematic topic like sacramentology, intercessory prayer, the sacrifice of the mass (and since I was Lutheran at the time, what was *wrong* with the sacrifice of the mass), etc. That is the way academic theology usually treats liturgy: from the heights of the ivory tower it shines the light of scholarly analysis upon liturgy the same way it shines it on various other topics on the landscape below. In addition to Chalcedon, Chrysostom, and Calvin, in addition to bible, morality, and sin, some theologian might choose (for who knows what personal reason) to study worship. The output is a text for the next generation of scholars to read and critique.

Schmemann and Kavanagh went about things differently, and I immodestly admit my pleasure in seeing my name occasionally added to theirs, if only for the reason of trying to explain the ramifications of the shift they promoted. Instead of thinking that liturgical theology springs from the

head of an academic, like Athena sprang from the head of
Zeus, they thought liturgical theology is the theology that
happens in the liturgy. This means that liturgical theology is
something the academy *receives*, it is not something the
academy *produces*. Liturgical theology does not admit of a
single author, it claims an origin that Kavanagh describes as
proletarian, not elitist; communitarian, not idiosyncratic;
quotidian, not random or infrequent; and that has a certain
violence about it. He underscores Schmemann's point that
"Liturgy is not one locus among many, but the condition of
doing theology."[162] If there is any author of liturgical
theology, it is the Holy Spirit, and he does not use the tools
of keyboard and screen, but the tools of assembly, icon,
incense, procession, sacramental matter, sacrificial oblation,
posture, gesture, symbol, architecture, chant, art, rubric, ritual
cult, ordered ceremony, and pneumatic charism. A liturgical
act is not just the pious straw of simple believers awaiting an
academic Rumpelstiltskin to spin it into real theological gold.

When the liturgy is in motion it throws off theology, like a grinding wheel throws off sparks. Liturgical theology arises from the Church's regular encounter with God, which occurs at the altar of the Lord where heaven and earth meet in the priesthood of Christ. After God has theologically shaped the community in liturgical encounter, the liturgiologist can dust the ritual for God's fingerprints and observe the structural evolution of rites, which will help the secondary theologian understand what went on. But liturgical theology first materializes upon the encounter with the Holy One at this altar, and although an academic can go back to his desk in the office to analyze what happened, the former is primary and the latter is secondary.

This is the foundation, as poured during my graduate studies. It is the basis upon which I have tried to build ever since, and the house I have constructed has three floors, so far. The first floor is an enlarged definition of liturgy. If liturgy were simply the organizational etiquette at a meeting of the Jesus Club, then the *lex orandi* cannot establish the Church's *lex credendi* because liturgy would be our self-expression. The second floor is an enlarged definition of theology that has personal and existential consequence. And the third floor is my most recent addition: liturgical asceticism, which capacitates a person to do mundane liturgy. I thought this was my innovation, but on retrospect I discover Kavanagh was there ahead of me when he would offer his definition of liturgy as "doing the world the way the world was meant to be done."

1. A Theological Definition of Liturgy

It is true that liturgy involves people, so you could give it an anthropological definition; it is true that liturgy involves a group of people, so you could give it a sociological definition; it is true that those people do ceremonial actions, so you could give it a ritual studies definition; but what if liturgy is not self-generated expression, but a responsive-expression to an act of God? Then we would enter a theological definition of liturgy. This is significant, because if liturgy was nothing more than the "work of the people," as is sometimes innocently said, then we would be suggesting that *lex credendi* stands upon man, while it is evident that the law of belief must stand upon God. If liturgy is an expression of human religiosity, then we would be grounding theology upon ourselves, upon our own outlook, and then the phrase *lex orandi statuat lex credendi* becomes a mere tautology: the prayer we choose to do becomes the basis of the theology we choose to believe.

In order to grasp the definition of liturgical theology there must be a different quality to liturgy, and I think to call this quality "sacramental" because it parallels the miracle by which human and empirical actions convey a reality that can only come from God. Colman O'Neil describes this by saying "The Church's visible act of sacramental worship is taken over by Christ and given value of sanctification quite beyond what it possesses as an act of Church worship."[163] I make the following application: the Church's visible act of liturgy is taken over by Christ and given a value quite beyond what you see the human beings doing. Kavanagh put in my student hands an article from Paul Holmer who makes the point this way: "liturgy is not an expression of how people see things; rather it proposes, instead, how God sees all people. It may seem an exaggeration to suggest it, but, strictly speaking, liturgy is no more an invention nor a human device to get hold of God than is the gospel itself."[164]

The starting point of liturgy is God himself, not ourselves, a point recalled by the pioneers of the liturgical movement. I will select only Virgil Michel as my witness, who puts it succinctly.

"The liturgy, through Christ, comes from the Father, the eternal source of the divine life in the Trinity. It in turn addresses itself in a special way to the Father, rendering him the homage and the glory of which it is capable through the power of Christ. The flow of divine life between the eternal Father and the Church is achieved and completed through the operation of the Holy Ghost.

The liturgy, reaching from God to man, and connecting man to the fullness of the Godhead, is the action of the Trinity in the Church. The Church in her liturgy partakes of the life of the divine society of the three persons in God."[165]

The Trinity is at work in this enlarged, theological understanding of liturgy. After a long and therapeutical pedagogy of the human race across salvation history, the first person of the Trinity accomplished the mystery of his will by making the second person of the Trinity incarnate through the third person of the Trinity. This was the Paschal Mystery, given to mankind to live by in the final aeon, the age of the Church. This new life can only be unleashed personally by the resurrected Christ, which is why *Sacrosanctum Concilium* says, "To accomplish so great a work, Christ is always present in

His Church, especially in her liturgical celebrations. ...
Rightly, then, the Liturgy is considered as an exercise of the
Priestly Office of Jesus Christ" (paragraph 7). *Leitourgia*
originally meant a public work, or what Schmemann says is
the work of a few on behalf of the many. Liturgy is the
Paschal work of Christ on behalf of the humanity he
assumed, and every baby liturgist born in the font of baptism
becomes his apprentice in serving this gift of life to the
world.[166] Though Christ has ascended, he continues his high
priesthood at the right hand of the Father, uniting heaven and
earth, leading me to say "There are not two liturgies, one in
heaven and one on earth; there is one liturgy, in heaven and
on earth."

In this thickened definition of liturgy one can sense
the meaning of de Lubac's famous phrase that "the Eucharist
makes the Church." Certainly the Church celebrates the
sacramental liturgies, but it is God who is constructing
Christians through them. We cannot bring ourselves to life,

but a God active-in-liturgy calls forth this resurrected humanity, called the Church, and it is his law of doxology that establishes her *lex credendi*. In the liturgy we absorb the light of Mount Tabor so that we can shine a theological light on the cosmos. Liturgy does not have a conflict with the world, it only has a conflict with worldliness, because worldliness has let that theological light in our eye go out. But when it is rekindled, then the eyebeam of the Christian sees that food is for Eucharist, and not simply something to eat and drink merrily until we die. It sees that matter is raw material for an eternal temple, and not a withering substance that will fold under the pressure of mortality. It sees an eschatological end that saves history from being a meaningless circling round nothingness. It sees that our fundamental nature is doxological, and that we do violence to ourselves when we act as idolaters. It sees our neighbor as companion, and not competitor – and even more incredibly, it sees God as companion, and not competitor. Peace on earth has been established.

2. A Liturgical Definition of Theology

We ascend now to the second floor up a staircase made of a series of steps. First, liturgy is theology in motion; second, liturgy is sacramental in the sense that it is an action of God occurring in the rite done by human beings; third, the Word of God can be liturgically inscribed upon us; and fourth, we reach the level at which theology receives a new definition. Tomas Spidlik says that the Eastern fathers "understood the practice of theology only as a personal communion with *Theos*, the Father, through the *Logos*, Christ, in the Holy Spirit – an experience lived in a state of prayer."[167] Liturgical theology concerns deification. In the liturgy, the Logos imprints himself upon a person, and since he is the mediator he brings us into personal relationship with the Father. Theology is union that comes about in prayer, as

Evagrius of Pontus bluntly asserts: "If you are a theologian you truly pray. If you truly pray you are a theologian."[168]

Evagrius summarized the ascetical process in three stages, the first active, the second two contemplative. The first stage he calls *praktike*, for it is attentive struggle with temptations so they do not take hold in us. Because this struggle is disciplined it was called *askesis*, which meant a kind of training. The word was first used of athletic training, and was soon applied to spiritual training. Praktike is learning to employ the faculties of human nature correctly, because if we do not, they become what the West called vices and the East called passions. We never leave this stage behind, of course, but eventually it becomes sturdy enough to open out onto the contemplative life. *Praktike* gives birth to what Evagrius called *apatheia*, or dispassion, which is keeping control of three faculties of appetite, ire, and intellect. John Cassian translated *apatheia* as *puritas cordis*, purity of heart. And from that purity, Evagrius says, comes a child called *agape* who keeps the door to a deep knowledge, a contemplative knowledge of two things. One is the physical world, the cosmos as seen in the light of revelation, so Evagrius names this *physike*, and it is the second stage. It is a spiritual knowledge, because one sees beyond appearances to know the Creator in the signs of his creatures. But there is a final stage, which involves knowing the Creator directly. This is not knowledge about God, it is knowledge that comes by union with God. This stage is participation in the life of the Trinity; it is effortless and beatific; it consists of a supreme and steady regarding of the Godhead. Evagrius therefore names this third stage *theologia*. Here theology is defined as communion rather than cogitation.

Yves Congar wrote a piece that started out as an entry for a French Dictionary of Theology, but outgrew its word limit, so was published under the title "History of Theology." It is not a history of the content of theology, it is a history of how the word "theology" has been used, and in it Congar says "we must wait for Abelard before the term *theologia* receives the meaning it has for us."[169] Until that point, he says, even in the West theology meant a divine science that included a kind of participation. It was "experimental," in the sense that it made meaning from direct experience (from *experiri*: to test, to try). *Theologia* counsels us to taste and see. Congar writes that for the Fathers theology "means a knowledge of God which is either the highest form of the gnosis or of that illumination of the soul by the Holy Spirit which is more than an effect since it is the very substance of its divinization or godlike transformation. ... In short, it is that perfect knowledge of God which is identified with the summit of prayer."[170] To pray is to be a theologian, to be a theologian is to pray, not because academics should look up from their manuscripts to take an occasional prayer break, but because theology is about deification, union with God.

This ascetical definition of *theologia* as being filled with the deifying Spirit of God explains how Kavanagh can call

Mrs. Murphy a theologian. Kavanagh uses Mrs. Murphy as a personification of somebody who has been formed by the rule of liturgical prayer, i.e., by *lex orandi,* and this formation creates a theologian. She is formed in the image of Jesus while submitting to the discipline of the liturgical year, the liturgy of the hours, the Divine Liturgy, liturgical sacraments and sacramentals. Theology is pneumatic communion with *Theos* through *Logos.* We can hardly call Mrs. Murphy a theologian if by that term we mean someone who has completed an advanced academic degree, but what if you do not *learn* theology, what if you *become* theology? Archimandrite Vasileios says "True theology is always living, a form of hierugy, something that changes our life and 'assumes' us into itself: we are to become theology. Understood in this way, theology is not a matter for specialists but a universal vocation; each is called to become a 'theologian soul.'"[171] In that case, the liturgical theologian can be understood to be doing *theologia prima.* Kavanagh writes,

"Mrs. Murphy is, as a consequence of her baptism, a primary theologian enjoying membership in that theological corporation Paul calls Christ's body, the church.

But the theological lingo she and her colleagues speak is not the same as that spoken by secondary theologians in academe. My professional language more often than not consist in words about words and concepts, and I wield them to test propositions which may then yield precision. The language of the primary theologian, however, more often consists in symbolic, metaphorical, sacramental words and actions which throw flashes of light upon chasms of rich ambiguity. As such, Mrs. Murphy's language illuminates the chaotic landscape through which I must pick my professional way with narrow laser-like beam of precise words about words and concepts – which is why what she does is primary and what I do is secondary; which is why, also, what she does is so much harder to do than what I do."[172]

Metropolitan Hierotheos gathers a bouquet of such definitions of theology from authors of the Philokalia. Maximus the Confessor says the Holy Spirit initiates a purified mind into the mysteries of the age to come, and the Metropolitan observes, "in this way the person becomes a theologian. For theology is not given by human knowledge and zeal, but by the work of the Holy Spirit which dwells in the pure heart."[173] Nicetas Stethatos says the mind that has been purified has the sun of righteousness shining in it, and it sends the beaming rays of theology out into the world, and so the Metropolitan concludes we may say "that his whole life, even his body itself, is theology. The purified man is wholly a theology."[174]

This is the connection that explains Schmemann's otherwise enigmatic and startling claim that "in the approach which I advocate by every line I ever wrote, the question addressed by liturgical theology to liturgy and to the entire liturgical tradition is not about liturgy but about 'theology,' i.e. about the faith of the Church as expressed, communicated and preserved by the liturgy."[175] Schmemann, famed as a liturgical theologian, says that he did not write about liturgy! When he wrote about liturgy he was writing about theology as the faith of the Church. Therefore, he bemoans the mutual isolation of liturgy from theology and from piety, and says "the goal of liturgical theology, as its very name indicates, is to overcome the fateful divorce between theology, liturgy and piety – a divorce which, as we have already tried to show elsewhere, has had disastrous consequences for theology as well as for liturgy and piety."[176] Liturgical theology is not an academic theology about liturgy, it is the reunification of theology, liturgy, and piety (that last I am calling the results of asceticism). Let these drift apart, and liturgy becomes ceremony, theology becomes an intellectual exercise, and piety loses its term of reference. He labels this as the fundamental flaw of scholasticism, the blame for which he lays at the feet of the West. "It is indeed to the 'original sin' of the entire Western theological development that it made 'texts' the only *loci theologici*, the extrinsic 'authorities' of theology, disconnecting theology from its living source: liturgy and spirituality."[177] "I always come to the same conclusion: [what is absolute in Orthodoxy] is first of all a certain vision, an experience of God, the world, the man. The best in Orthodox theology is about that vision…"[178]

Our vision usually takes in more than we can describe. Even in ordinary perception, the epistemologist Michael Polanyi remarks that "we know more than we can say." The tacit is that realm of silence where a different knowledge is generated. I think Andrew Louth's words applies that insight to spiritual knowledge when he says this silence of the tacit is "the silence of presence, the presence of God who gives himself to the soul who waits on him in silence. The silence of the tacit makes immediate contact with the silence of prayer: and prayer is seen in the Fathers to be, as it were, the amniotic fluid in which our knowledge of God takes form."[179] If I say "liturgy generates theology," I will be misunderstood so long as we categorize theology as a an activity of ratiocination. I mean that liturgy generates theology the way a womb births a baby. Liturgy is where we can today climb Mount Moriah with a faith willing to sacrifice our dearest possession, where we can cast off our sandals before the burning bush to stand on holy ground, where we can exit on dry ground across the Red Sea from Satan's slavery and enter on dry ground across the Jordan River into the promised land, where we can expect hearts of stone to be made into flesh, where we can dance in our priestly vestment accompanying the ark to the holy mountain, where we can find waters to wash off our leprosy, where we can burn up our own personal gods of Baal on Mount Carmel when the prophet makes his epiclesis and Pentecost fire descends upon our lives, where we can dwell in God's tabernacle and rest in his holy hill (Psalm 14) because the soldier has thrust his lance into Christ's side and brought forth his bride while he slept in death – and if liturgy is this sort of place, I say, then it produces theology because it produces deified persons, theologian souls.

3. A Liturgical Theology of the World

Those are my first two floors. On the first I found that liturgy had thickened into *leitourgia,* and on the second I found that theology had thickened into *theologia.* I had begun to learn an unusual grammar, one that claimed we join a liturgy already in progress, activated by the activity of the Holy Trinity; that the Church is more than the Jesus club and her liturgical activity is divinely inspired; that we are made theologian souls and that our very body becomes theology; that Mrs. Murphy knows more than the academic can define; that theology is experimental. What awaited me on the third floor?

We are not often lucky enough to have an author be self-conscious of the genesis of a concept, but Kavanagh was aware of the first time he saw liturgical theology this way, and provides an account in a 1983 lecture to *Societas Liturgica* titled "Liturgy and Ecclesial Consciousness." In it he quotes the response of Metropolitan Anthony Bloom to an interviewer who accused Bloom of presiding over his liturgies without emotion, with almost mechanical execution. Bloom replied that this was actually the result of constant work over many years. He said to the interviewer,

> "We have to get rid of emotions...in order to reach...feeling. There is a profound logic [in the liturgy] ... And this logic leads people somewhere – without their knowing it intellectually. ... For this you have to be in a state of prayer, otherwise it passes you by. ... In the state of prayer one is *vulnerable* ... not enthusiastic. And then these rituals have such force. They hit you like a locomotive. You must not be

enthusiastic, nor rejecting – but only open. This is the whole aim of asceticism: to become open. [Ellipses in original]"[180]

Kavanagh says he had personally experienced this when he attended a liturgy in Metropolitan Anthony's London cathedral ("which was celebrated in full pontificals assisted only by two small servers and one large nun").

"I can witness to its superb popular affectiveness: it was a theophany of the Creator being praised for no other reason than for himself.

It hit me like a locomotive. It was a superb act of proclamation, of sacrifice, of ministry precisely because it was just so ascetical an act of public worship. It was at this time that I first began to experience the fact that the act of Christian liturgy is the premier theological act of a believing community as it stands before the living God. ... It is this reconciliation which the same community proclaims as good news in the world. It is not a program, not an

ethic, not a political theory, not an ideology. It is as

near to a description of, and a summons into, the

world renovated according to God's pleasure as

exists. It is the world seen in the light of Christ's

gospel."[181]

Liturgy is the premier theological act. It is made by a

believing community in public worship that praises God for

being God, and for no other reason. When God, who is

mercy, acts as God, he reconciles his estranged people and

this is the gospel that the liturgical community (otherwise

known as the Church) carries into the world. That gospel

weighs on their hearts until they proclaim it, and thus liturgy

is the font of evangelization. That gospel weighs on their

hearts until they are conformed to Jesus, and thus liturgy is

the font of conversion. That gospel weighs on their hearts

until a fallen world is lifted up, a broken world is repaired, an

estranged world is reconciled, a dead world is brought to life, and thus liturgy is the font of ministry. That is why Kavanagh defined liturgy as "doing the world the way the world was meant to be done." Now liturgy breaks out of its ritual womb to consecrate the world.

Liturgy is all-embracing, cosmic in scope and eschatological in ambition. Liturgy does not just give us a place to go on Sunday morning, it gives us a place to go finally: I mean, to the throne of the Lamb at judgment day. Liturgy does not just give us a thing to do on Sunday morning, it prescribes our daily task: all moments become oblation. Our liturgical companions are not just our friends in the Jesus club, they are the Church of the righteous pagan, the Church of the Old Testament, the Church militant, the Church suffering, the Church glorious, the angels and archangels. Liturgy trails after Jesus because the Son's life is liturgical. Liturgy is praise of God, and the Eternal Son, who praised the Father with his divine voice, now adds a second and human voice, like a Tibetan throat singer. His human voice is united to his divine voice without confusion, separation, change, or division. More incredibly, our own human voice now finds itself combined with his so that the liturgy that comes out of our mouth is Christ's, carried on the breath of the Holy Spirit. This is a consequence of deification: our liturgy is no longer only our own. Liturgy is human ritual in the way that Jesus was man: fully, but not only.

My own definition of liturgy has had to wait for this floor of the house. Liturgy is *"the perichoresis of the Trinity kenotically extended to invite our synergistic ascent into deification."*[182] In other words, the circulation of love shared in mutual reciprocity by the persons of the Trinity is turned outward in an act of creation. But creation is only the beginning of redemption, as redemption is only the completion of creation. The Son and Spirit descend kenotically to enact the Father's pleasure for all creation, which is nothing less than to invite us to ascend and participate in the very life of the

Trinity, which is our deification. But this cannot be forced; it must be done with our cooperation. We are talking about an ontological mystery stretched taut between alpha and omega, one that does not just concern the Church but is God's plan for the whole world. That is the Mystery upon which creation rests, and the Mystery that the Church breathes in order to live. Paul describes it in his letter to the Ephesians.

I imagine the book of Ephesians to be St. Paul writing his response to the final exam question: "Why did God create? Be complete in your answer." He gives it in three parts. First he says that this is an eternal plan that has always existed in the mind of the Father. "He chose us before the foundation of the world to be holy and without blemish" and "he destined us for adoption" (Chapter 1:4-5). From before the big bang God intended to adopt us into the perichoresis of the holy Trinity. Second, Paul says the Father's will came to pass through Jesus Christ, in whose blood we have been redeemed (1:7). The riches of the Father's grace have been lavished upon us, and "he has made known to us the mystery of his will... As a plan for the fullness of times, to sum up all things in Christ, in heaven and earth" (Chapter 1:9-10).The Son's incarnation makes known the Father's mystery the way a carpenter makes known the architect's blueprint. Third, Paul says this mystery also involves us. "In him we were also chosen, destined in accord with the purpose of the One who accomplishes all things according to the intention of his will, so that we might exist for the praise of his glory" (Chapter 1:11). We are natural liturgists. Liturgy is our reason for existence. Doxology is the key to ontology. Man and woman were created to be cosmic priests, the fall is the forfeiture of our liturgical career, and redemption is being baptized into the New Adam's liturgical state.

When John Chrysostom wrote his own final exam (titled his homilies on Ephesians) he exclaimed:

"Strange! What Friendship! For [God] tells us His secrets; the mysteries ... of his will, as if one should say, He has made known to us *the things that are in His heart.* For here is indeed the mystery which is full of all wisdom and prudence. ... [T]his He desired, this He travailed for, as one might say, that He might be able to reveal to us the mystery. What mystery? *That He would have man seated up on high.* And this has come to pass."[183]

We are created in the image of God to grow into the likeness of God, and be seated up on high, and by the Holy Spirit join the Son's glorification of the Father. Why, it almost seems as if the Church was not made for the world, but the world was made for the Church. Indeed, so said the Shepherd of Hermas, quoted in paragraph 760 of the Catechism of the Catholic Church:

> ""The world was created for the sake of the Church" [*Pastor Hermae*]. God created the world for the sake of communion with his divine life, a communion brought about by the "convocation" of men in Christ,

and this "convocation" is the Church. The Church is the goal of all things [St Epiphanius] and God permitted such painful upheavals as the angels' fall and man's sin only as occasions and means for displaying all the power of his arm in the whole measure of the love he wanted to give the world. Just as God's will is creation and is called "the world," so his intention is the salvation of men, and it is called "the Church" [Clement of Alexandria]".

This plan of God can be called the Mystery; it is the Father's plan for non-divine creatures to join in the perichoresis; it is the communion of human beings with God; Jesus' hypostatic union is the Mystery in the flesh, when the Son pitched his tent among us (John 1:14); this is the world's teleology, the New Adam done right, the end for which man and woman were made; deification is our telos, and when we are lifted up and seated on high to share in God's own divine life, as John Chrysostom says, we bring creation with us. Our promised

Ascension is not an escape hatch out of the world, it is the one, holy, catholic and apostolic parade of the cosmos coming home. Liturgy is the *consecration of the world*.

Pope Paul VI clarifies that this does not mean carving the world in two, and discarding the profane in favor of the sacred. Quite the contrary. "Let it suffice here to recall that by consecration we mean, not the separation of a thing from what is profane in order to reserve it exclusively, or particularly, for the Divinity, but, in a wider sense, the reestablishment of the thing's relationship to God according to its own order, according to the exigency of the nature of the thing itself, in the plan willed by God."[184] By world he means "the set of natural, positive values, which are in the temporal order." It is what *Gaudium et Spes* defines as the whole human family, along with the sum of the realities in which it lives. It is what Schmemann means when he says the world is that in which and by which we live. And to consecrate the world is to reestablish all this in its proper relationship to God. That means overcoming the passions so that we do not misuse the world. The lesson taught us by asceticism is that there is nothing wrong with the world, but any thing in the world can be used wrongly. Consecration of the world requires an ascetical foundation, but it further requires a liturgical logic. Consecrating the world was the priestly activity for which Adam and Eve were created, which they forfeited, and which the New Adam has given to the Church, his New Eve.

This is the liturgical agenda given to Christians for the cosmos. This agenda is celebrated in sacramental liturgy and lived in cosmic liturgy. Pope Benedict XVI affirmed this in his 2008 homily at the Solemnity of the Holy Apostles Peter and Paul when he refers to St. Paul's letter to the Romans, chapter 15.

"[St. Paul] speaks of the cosmic liturgy in which the human world itself must become worship of God, an oblation in the Holy Spirit. When the world in all its

parts has become a liturgy of God, when, in its reality,
it has become adoration, then it will have reached its
goal and will be safe and sound. This is the ultimate
goal of St Paul's apostolic mission as well as of our
own mission. The Lord calls us to this ministry. Let
us pray at this time that he may help us to carry it out
properly, to become true liturgists of Jesus Christ."[185]
Our purpose in life: to become true liturgists of Jesus Christ.
Or, in Schmemann's words, man and woman are created to
be *homo adorans*.

Grace is perfecting nature everywhere we look. Now
nothing in the world looks the same. To the naked, secular
eye nothing looks different, but to the sanctified, consecrated
eye every object and moment has a new potentiality. Once we
have seen God invite himself into the house of Zacchaeus for
supper, or stop for dinner in Emmaus after a long day's walk,
there is no meal which is purely secular. Once we have seen
Christ on the green hills of Galilee and the crowded streets of

Jerusalem, we privilege neither the pastoral nor the political. Once we have seen God on the cross there is no corner of suffering or darkness where our spiritual eyes do not see him moving. Once we have seen God in Hades, we know there is no length to which he will not go to find us.

In order to understand liturgical theology, I think we must know the origin of liturgy, and liturgy does not originate with our decision to gather as the Jesus Club. The origin of liturgy is a divine decision to summon a people, enter into covenant with them, train them in faith, hope, and love to conform to the incarnate one, place into their hands the Son's worship of the Father, sacramentally equip them to be icon and instrument of the kingdom, make them a theandric people by perpetuating the hypostatic union in their adoption, breathe in them sighs too deep for their human words, illuminate them in the light of Mount Tabor, let them drink from the currently invisible eschatological springs of life upon which history is carried, inspire them as prophetic witnesses in the face of a death-dealing culture, make all the baptized

concelebrants of the Church's mystical sacrifice, and fill them

with spiritual life, by which I mean the life of the Spirit. Then

we will have become true liturgists. And that is what occupies

the attention of liturgical theology.[186]

[1] Alexander Schmemann, "Liturgical Theology, Theology of Liturgy, and Liturgical Reform," in *Liturgy and Tradition*, ed. Thomas Fisch (Crestwood, NY: St. Vladimir Seminary Press, 1990) 46.
[2] Alexander Schmemann, "Theology and Liturgy," *The Greek Orthodox Theological Review, vol 17, No 1, Spring 1972*, 94. Reprinted in *Church, World, Mission* (Crestwood, NY: St. Vladimir's Seminary Press, 1997).
[3] Alexander Schmemann, *Of Water and the Spirit* (Crestwood, NY: St. Vladimir Seminary Press, 1974) 12. The reference he makes to having tried to show elsewhere is to his book, *Introduction to Liturgical Theology* (New York: St. Vladimir's Seminary Press, 1966).
[4] Alexander Schmemann, "Liturgy and Theology," in Fisch, 51-2.
[5] Alexander Schmemann, *Introduction to Liturgical Theology*, 25
[6] Alexander Schmemann, *The Journals of Father Alexander Schmemann* (Crestwood, NY: St. Vladimir's Seminary Press, 2002), 233
[7] Alexander Schmemann,, "Problems of Orthodoxy in America: III. The Spiritual Problem," *St. Vladimir's Seminary Quarterly,* vol 9, no 4, 1965, 173.
[8] Alexander Schmemann,, "Problems of Orthodoxy in America: II. The Liturgical Problem," *St. Vladimir's Seminary Quarterly,* vol 8, no. 4, 1964, 175.
[9] Schmemann, *Of Water and the Spirit*, 151
[10] Schmemann, *Journals*, 329-30
[11] Alexander Schmemann, "Ecclesiological Notes" St. Vladimir's

Seminary Quarterly, vol 11, no 1, 1967, 36.

[12] Schmemann, *For the Life of the World* (Crestwood, NY: St. Vladimir's Seminary Press, 1973) 23.

[13] Schmemann, *Journals*, 233.

[14] Pavel Florensky, *The Pillar and Ground of the Truth*, 108.

[15] *Ibid.*, 107

[16] *Ibid.*, 118.

[17] *Ibid.*

[18] Alexander Schmemann, *Journals*, 229.

[19] Schmemann, "Theology and Liturgy," 96.

[20] Alexander Schmemann, "The Missionary Imperative," in *Church, World, Mission,* 211-12

[21] Schmemann, *Journals*, 29

[22] Alexander Schmemann, "Prayer, Liturgy, and Renewal," in *The Greek Orthodox Theological Review*, 14, no 1, Spring 1969, 8. The same point is made with similar language here: "This is the experience of the Kingdom of God and not a mere doctrine 'de novissimis' – experience centered on the Church's self-fulfillment in the Eucharist, on the Lord's Day – that permeates the whole faith and the whole life of the early Church," and this "explains the antinomical character of that attitude, the correlation within it of an emphatic *yes* to the world with an equally emphatic *no*." "The 'Orthodox World,' Past and Present," in *Church, World, Mission*, 29.

[23] Schmemann, *The Eucharist*, 82.

[24] Schmemann, *Introduction to Liturgical Theology*, 80.

[25] Alexander Schmemann, "Theology and Eucharist," in Fisch, 79.

[26] Alexander Schmemann, "Fast and Liturgy: Notes in Liturgical Theology," *St. Vladimir Seminary Quarterly*, vol 3, no 1, 1959, 4.

[27] Alexander Schmemann, *Journals*, 329.

[28] Alexander Schmemann, "The Ecumenical Agony," in *Church, World, Mission*, 203.

[29] Alexander Schmemann, "The Underlying Question," in *Church World Mission*, 7.

[30] Alexander Schmemann, *Journals,* 234.

[31] (a) The task of theology is to be faithful to that antinomy; (b) that antinomy is experienced in the liturgy; (c) therefore the liturgy is the ontological condition for performing the task of faithful theology.

[32] Schmemann, "The Missionary Imperative," 216.

[33] Schmemann, "Theology and Eucharist," in Fisch, 79.

[34] Alexander Schmemann, "Freedom in the Church," in *Church, World, Mission*, 189.

[35] Schmemann, "Theology and Eucharist," in Fisch, 79.

[36] Schmemann, "Liturgy and Theology," in Fisch, 56.

[37] Schmemann, *Journals*, 274.

[38] Alexander Schmemann, "Prayer, Liturgy, and Renewal," *The Greek Orthodox Theological Review*, 14, no 1, Spring 1969, 11.

[39] Schmemann, "Problems of Orthodoxy in America: II. The Liturgical Problem," 185.

[40] Schmemann, *For the Life of the World*, 26-7.

[41] *Ibid.*, 112.

[42] Schmemann, "Problems of Orthodoxy in America: II. The Liturgical Problem," 173.

[43] Schmemann, "Liturgy and Eschatology," in Fisch, 95.

[44] Alexander Schmemann,, "The 'Orthodox World,' Past and Present," in *Church, World, Mission*, 30.

[45] Alexander Schmemann, *The Eucharist*, 53.

[46] Schmemann, "Problems of Orthodoxy in America: III The Spiritual Problem," 188.

[47] Schmemann, "The Missionary Imperative," 216.

[48] Robert Taft, "Liturgy as Theology," *Beyond East and West: Problems in Liturgical Understanding* (Rome: Pontifical Oriental Institute, 1997) 240.

[49] Alexander Schmemann, "Theology and Eucharist" in *Liturgy and Tradition: Theological Reflections of Alexander Schmemann*, ed. Thomas Fisch (Crestwood, NY: St. Vladimir's Seminary Press, 1990) 70.

[50] Schmemann, "Theology and Eucharist," in Fisch, 71.

[51] Alexander Schmemann, "The Underlying Question," in *Church, World, Mission* (Crestwood, NY: St. Vladimir Seminary Press, 1979) 22.

[52] Robert Taft, "Mrs. Murphy Goes to Moscow: Kavanagh, Schmemann, and 'The Byzantine Synthesis.'" *Worship* 85 (2011), 387.

[53] Alexander Schmemann, "Liturgy and Theology," in Fisch 95.

[54] Alexander Schmemann, "Theology and Liturgical Tradition," in Fisch, 11-12.

[55] Alexander Schmemann, "Liturgical Theology: Remarks on Method," in Fisch, 137.

[56] Alexander Schmemann, "Symbols and Symbolism in the Byzantine Liturgy: Liturgical Symbols and Their Theological Interpretation," in Fisch, 128.

[57] Schmemann, "Liturgical Theology: Remarks on Method," 137-38.

[58] Schmemann, "Theology and Eucharist," in Fisch, 87.

[59] Schmemann, "Theology and Liturgical Tradition," 18.

[60] *Ibid.*, 13.

[61] *Ibid.*, 14

[62] Schmemann, "Liturgy and Theology," 52.

[63] Alexander Schmemann, "Liturgical Movement and Orthodox Ecumenical Feeling: Alexander Schmemann," *American Benedictine Review*, vol 14, issue 2, 1963, 181-182.

[64] Alexander Schmemann, "In Memoriam: Vladimir Lossky," *St. Vladimir Seminary Quarterly*, vol 2, no 2, Spring 1958, 47.

[65] Schmemann, "Liturgy and Theology," 98.

[66] Alexander Schmemann, "The Task of Orthodox Theology in America Today," St. Vladimir's Seminary Quarterly, vol 10, no 4, 1966, 183.

[67] Tomas Spidlik, *The Spirituality of the Christian East*, (Kalamazoo, MI: Cistercian Press, 1986) 1.

[68] Archimandrite Vasileios, *Hymn of Entry: Liturgy and Life in the Orthodox Church* (Crestwood, NY: St. Vladimir's Seminary Press, 1984) 27.

[69] Schmemann, "Liturgy and Theology," 90.

[70] Schmemann, "The Underlying Question," 20.

[71] Alexander Schmemann, "Freedom in the Church," in *Church, World, Mission*, 188

[72] Alexander Schmemann, "Liturgical Theology, Theology of Liturgy, and Liturgical Reform," in Fisch, 42.

[73] Alexander Schmemann, *Introduction to Liturgical Theology* (New York: St. Vladimir's Seminary Press, 1975) 15.

[74] Alexander Schmemann, *Introduction to Liturgical Theology*, 15.

[75] Schmemann, "Theology and Liturgical Tradition," 13.

[76] Aidan Kavanagh describes Mrs. Murphy this way: "The language of the primary theologian ... more often consists in symbolic, metaphorical, sacramental words and actions which throw flashes of light upon chasms of rich ambiguity. As such, Mrs. Murphy's language illuminates the chaotic landscape through which I must pick my professional way with the narrow laser-like beam of precise words and concepts – which is why what she does is primary and what I do is secondary; which is why, also, what she does is so much harder to do than what I do. My admiration for her and her colleagues is profound, and it deepens daily." In "Response: Primary Theology and Liturgical Act," *Worship* 57, July 1983, 323.

[77] Schmemann, "Liturgy and Theology," 65.

[78] Alexander Schmemann, *The Journals of Father Alexander Schmemann 1973-1983* (Crestwood: St. Vladimir's Seminary Press, 2002) 13.

[79] *Ibid.*, 89.

[80] Richard Gustafson, introduction to Pavel Florensky, *The Pillar and Ground of the Truth*, (Princeton: Princeton University Press, 1997) xiv.

[81] David Fagerberg, "The Cost of Understanding Schmemann in the West," *St. Vladimir's Theological Quarterly*, Vol. 53, Numbers 2-3, 2009, 185.

[82] Schmemann, *The Journals*, 300.

[83] Alexander Schmemann, "Ecclesiological Notes," *St. Vladimir's Seminary Quarterly*, vol 11, no 1, 1967, 35.

[84] *Ibid.*, 37

[85] Schmemann, "Liturgical Theology, Theology of Liturgy, and Liturgical Reform," 38-9.

[86] As Schmemann defines it in a book review of *The Liturgy of the Presanctified* by D. N. Moraitis, *St Vladimir's Seminary Quarterly*, ns 1 no 2 Apr 1957, p 31-34 31

[87] Schmemann, "Liturgical Movement and Orthodox Ecumenical Feeling," 183-84.

[88] Alexander Schmemann, "Prayer, Liturgy, and Renewal," *The Greek Orthodox Theological Review*, 14, no 1, Spring 1969, 12.

[89] *Ibid.*

[90] Schmemann, "Prayer, Liturgy, and Renewal," 7.

[91] Schmemann, "Prayer, Liturgy, and Renewal," 13.

[92] Schmemann, "Prayer, Liturgy, and Renewal," 8.

[93] Schmemann, "Prayer, Liturgy, and Renewal," 9. See also his entire article titled "The World As Sacrament," in *Church, World, Mission* (Crestwood, NY: St. Vladimir Seminary Press, 1979).

[94] Alexander Schmemann, "The Missionary Imperative," in *Church, World, Mission*, 216.

[95] Alexander Schmemann, "Liturgy and Eschatology," in *Liturgy and Tradition: Theological Reflections of Alexander Schmemann*, ed. Thomas Fisch (Crestwood, NY: St. Vladimir's Seminary Press, 1990) 96.

[96] Schmemann, "Prayer, Liturgy, and Renewal," 10.

[97] Alexander Schmemann, "The 'Orthodox World,' Past and Present," in *Church, World, Mission*, 60.

[98] Alexander Schmemann, *Introduction to Liturgical Theology* (New York: St. Vladimir's Seminary Press, 1975), 12.

[99] Alexander Schmemann, *The Journals of Father Alexander Schmemann 1973-1983* (Crestwood: St. Vladimir's Seminary Press, 2002), 146.

[100] Alexander Schmemann, "Fast and Liturgy: Notes in Liturgical Theology," *St. Vladimir's Seminary Quarterly*, vol 3, no 1, 1959, 7-8.

[101] Alexander Schmemann, *Introduction to Liturgical Theology*, 22-3

[102] Alexander Schmemann, "Worship in a Secular Age," *St. Vladimir's Theological Quarterly*, vol 16, no 1, 1972, 13

[103] Alexander Schmemann, "Theology and Eucharist," 79.

[104] Schmemann, "Prayer, Liturgy, and Renewal," 12.

[105] *Ibid.*, 12-13.

[106] Alexander Schmemann, "Liturgical Theology: Remarks on Method," in Fisch 143.

[107] Schmemann, "Prayer, Liturgy, and Renewal," 15-16.

[108] *Ibid.*

[109] Alexander Schmemann, "Fast and Liturgy," 7-8.

[110] Schmemann, *Introduction to Liturgical Theology*, 12.

[111] Alexander Schmemann, "Theology and Liturgical Tradition" in Fisch, 16-17,

[112] Alexander Schmemann, "Problems of Orthodoxy in America: II. The Liturgical Problem," *St. Vladimir's Seminary Quarterly*, vol 8, no 2, 1964, 179.

[113] Alexander Schmemann, *Of Water and the Spirit* (Crestwood, NY: St. Vladimir's Seminary Press, 1974) 83.

[114] *Ibid.*, 84

[115] Alexander Schmemann, "The World As Sacrament," in *Church, World, Mission*, 225-26

[116] Schmemann, "The Missionary Imperative," 213

[117] This can be found in Fagerberg, *On Liturgical Asceticism* (Washington DC: Catholic University Press of America, 2013.

[118] "In America, we often see the reduction of Orthodoxy to icons, to ancient singing, to Mt. Athos books about spiritual life. Byzantium is triumphing without a cosmic dimension. I can't avoid thinking that it is all a sort of romanticism – a love for that image of Orthodoxy, love because that image is radically different from the images of the contemporary world. Escape, departure, reduction of Orthodoxy." Alexander Schmemann, *The Journals*, 268.

[119] Alexander Schmemann, "The 'Orthodox World,' Past and Present," 49.

[120] Alexander Schmemann, "The World As Sacrament," in *Church, World, Mission*, 220.

[121] Schmemann, *Introduction to Liturgical Theology*, 138.

[122] Alexander Schmemann, "Problems Orthodoxy in America: III. The Spiritual Problem," *St. Vladimir's Seminary Quarterly*, vol. 9, no 4, 1965, 179-80.

[123] Alexander Schmemann, "The Ecumenical Agony," in *Church, World, Mission*, 206-7.

[124] Alexander Schmemann, "Problems Orthodoxy in America: II. The

Liturgical Problem," 165.

[125] Schmemann, "The Missionary Imperative," 216

[126] The phrase has become common, and it might be traced to Fr Ion Bria, "The Liturgy after the Liturgy," *International Review of Mission*, 1978, and reappearing in his book *The Liturgy after the Liturgy: Mission and Witness from an Orthodox Perspective* (Geneva: World Council of Churches, 1996).

[127] Alexander Schmemann, *For the Life of the World*, 15.

[128] *Ibid.*, 17.

[129] Alexander Schmemann, "The World As Sacrament," in *Church, World, Mission*, 223

[130] Schmemann, *Of Water and the Spirit*, 96

[131] Alexander Schmemann, "Sacrifice and Worship," in Fisch, 132

[132] Alexander Schmemann, "The Missionary Imperative," in *Church, World, Mission*, 215

[133] Schmemann, *Of Water and the Spirit*, 12.

[134] Alexander Schmemann, "Liturgy and Theology" in Fisch, 50.

[135] *Ibid.*, 89-90

[136] Schmemann, "Liturgical Theology: Remarks on Method," 142

[137] Schmemann, "Prayer, Liturgy, Renewal," 11.

[138] Pius XII, Mediator Dei, paragraph 25.

[139] Romano Guardini, "A Letter from Romano Guardini," *Herder Correspondence* (August 1964).

[140] Anthony Ruff, *Sacred Music and Liturgical Reform: Treasures and Transformations* (Chicago: Liturgical Training Publications, Hillenbrand Books, 2007) 213.

[141] David Fagerberg, "The Sacraments As Actions of the Mystical Body," *Communio*, vol. 39, No. 4, Winter 2012, 554-568.

[142] Alexander Schmemann, "The World As Sacrament" in *Church, World, Mission* (Crestwood, NY: St. Vladimir's Seminary Press, 1979) 225-26 .

[143] David Fagerberg, "An Academic Horror Story," *The Cresset*, Volume 60, Number 8, Michaelmas 1997, 15-17.

[144] Origen, in Jean Danielou, *The Angels and Their Mission* (Westminster, MD: Christian Classics, Inc., 1982) 28.

[145] Irenaeus, in Danielou, *The Angels and Their Mission*, 39.

[146] Gregory Nazianzen, in Danielou, *The Angels and Their Mission,* 41.

[147] Pope John Paul II, *Orientale Lumen.* Text in *Origins* 25: 1 (May 18, 1995), 87.

[148] *The Rules of Benedict*, chapter 31 (Collegeville, MN: *The Liturgical Press*, 1981) 229.

[149] C. S. Lewis, *Prince Caspian* in *The Chronicles of Narnia* (New

York: HarperCollins Books, 2001) 411.

[150] *Ibid.*, 347.

[151] Gilbert K. Chesterton, *The Everlasting Man*, in *G. K. Chesterton Collected Works*, vol. 2 (San Francisco: Ignatius, 1986), 242.

[152] Maximus the Confessor, "Four Hundred Chapters on Love," I.66, in *Maximus Confessor: Selected Writings* (Paulist Press, 1985) 42.

[153] Evagrius, *Praktike* 14, in John Etudes Bamberger, OCSO, ed., *The Pratikos & Chapters on Prayer* (Kalamazoo: Cistercian Publications, 1981) 20.

[154] Joseph Ratzinger, "The New Evangelization, http://www.ewtn.com/new_evangelization/Ratzinger.htm

[155] Joseph Ratzinger, *The Spirit of the Liturgy* (San Francisco: Ignatius Press, 2000), 32-33.

[156] Ratzinger, *The Spirit of the Liturgy,* 33.

[157] Paul Claudel, *Lord, Teach us to Pray* (London: Dennis Dobson, 1942) 8.

[158] *Ibid.*, 19, 29.

[159] Alexander Schmemann, "Theology and Liturgical Tradition," *Worship in Scripture and Tradition*, ed. Massey Shepherd (Oxford: Oxford University Press, 1963), 175.

[160] Aidan Kavanagh, *On Liturgical Theology*, (New York: Pueblo Publishing, 1984) 74.

[161] Kavanagh, *On Liturgical Theology*, 91.

[162] *Ibid.*, 88.

[163] Colman O'Neill, O.P., *Meeting Christ in the Sacraments* (New York: Society of St. Paul/Alba House, 1991) 119.

[164] Paul Holmer, "About Liturgy and Its Logic," Worship 50, No. 1 January, 1976, 22-23.

[165] Virgil Michel, *The Liturgy of the Church, According to the Roman Rite (New York: Macmillan, 1937). 40.*

[166] This is summarized in the definition of liturgy in the catechism of the Catholic Church, paragraph 1069: "The word 'liturgy' originally meant a 'public work' or a 'service in the name of/on behalf of the people.' In Christian tradition it means the participation of the People of God in 'the work of God.' Through the liturgy Christ, our Redeemer and high priest, continues the work of our redemption in, with, and through his Church."

[167] Tomas Spidlik, *The Spirituality of the Christian East* (Kalamazoo, MI: Cistercian Press, 1986) 1.

[168] Evagrius, *The Praktikos & Chapters on Prayer* (Kalamazoo: Cistercian Publications, 1981), p. 65.

[169] Yves Congar, *A History of Theology* (Garden City, NY: Doubleday

1968) 32.

[170] Ibid., 31. Thomas only uses the term three times in the summa, usually preferring sacra doctrina, which occurs about eighty times.

[171] Archimandrite Vasileios, *Hymn of Entry: Liturgy and Life in the Orthodox Church* (Crestwood: St. Vladimir's Seminary Press, 1984) 27.

[172] Aidan Kavanagh, "Response: Primary Theology and Liturgical Act," *Worship* 57 (July 1983) 323.

[173] Metropolitan Hierotheos, *Orthodoxy Psychotherapy: The Science of the Fathers* (Levadia: Birth of the Theotokos Monastery, 1994) 147.

[174] Ibid.

[175] Alexander Schmemann, "Liturgical Theology, Theology of Liturgy, and Liturgical Reform," in *Liturgy and Tradition*, ed. Thomas Fisch (Crestwood, NY: SVS Press. 1990) 40.

[176] Alexander Schmemann, *Of Water and the Spirit* (Crestwood: St. Vladimir's Seminary Press, 1974) 12.

[177] Schmemann, "Liturgical Theology, Theology of Liturgy, and Liturgical Reform," 42.

[178] Alexander Schmemann, *The Journals of Father Alexander Schmemann* (Crestwood, NY: St. Vladimir's Seminary Press, 2002), 89.

[179] Andrew Louth, *Discerning the Mystery* (New York: Oxford University Press, 1983) 65.

[180] Aidan Kavanagh, "Liturgy and Ecclesial Consciousness," *Studia Liturgica* 15.1 (January, 1982) quoting Metropolitan Bloom, 10. The Bloom quote comes from Jacob Needleman, *Lost Christianity* (New York: 1980) 24-25.

[181] Ibid., 11.

[182] David Fagerberg, *On Liturgical Asceticism* (Washington DC: Catholic University Press of America, 2013) 9.

[183] John Chrysostom, Homily 1 on Ephesians 1:1-3. Emphases added.

[184] Pope Paul VI, General audience April 23, 1969, "Layman Should Be World's Perfect Citizen." http://www.ewtn.com/library/PAPALDOC/P6LAYMAN.HTM

[185] Benedict XVI, "Homilies of His Holiness Bartholomew I and His Holiness Pope Benedict XVI, http://w2.vatican.va/content/benedict-xvi/en/homilies/2008/documents/hf_ben-xvi_hom_20080629_pallio.html

[186] Are there any more floors awaiting construction? I have drawn up blueprints for two more: liturgical dogmatics, and liturgical mysticism.

94441922R00132

Made in the USA
Middletown, DE
20 October 2018